THE WORLD ART TOUR

Sculpture

Architecture
Clothing and Fashion
Culinary Arts
Dance
Decorative Arts
Drawing and Painting
Festivals
Sculpture

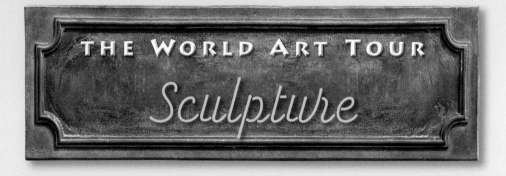

THE WORLD ART TOUR
Sculpture

BY Amy Sterling Casil

MASON CREST
Philadelphia • Miami

Mason Crest
450 Parkway Drive, Suite D
Broomall, PA 19008
(866) MCP-BOOK (toll free)
www.masoncrest.com

Printed in the United States of America

First printing
9 8 7 6 5 4 3 2 1

Series ISBN: 978-1-4222-4283-4
Hardcover ISBN: 978-1-4222-4291-9
E-book ISBN: 978-1-4222-7538-2

Cataloging-in-Publication Data is available on file
at the Library of Congress.

Developed and Produced by Print Matters Productions, Inc.
(www.printmattersinc.com)

Cover and Interior Design by Tom Carling, Carling Design, Inc.

CONTENTS

INTRODUCTION

Sculpture is a form of visual art created in three dimensions. Sculptures can be formed from nearly any material, but the earliest known sculpture materials were bone, stone, and wood. We may have an incorrect view of all the types of sculpture that have been made because stone is much more durable than wood or fiber. Thus, many early examples may be lost to time. The oldest known sculpture is the 40,000-year-old Lion-Man of the Hohlenstein-Stadel, carved from a mammoth tusk.

Early civilizations like Egypt and Assyria produced monumental sculptures and structures that glorified their rulers, considered to be living gods. The ancient Egyptians created massive monuments that have lasted for thousands of years, including the Great Pyramid and Sphinx of Giza.

Ancient Greeks created simple stone statues of idealized young men and women called *kouros* and *kore*, which were painted in vivid colors. As Greek democracy evolved in Athens, Greek sculpture achieved a realism and dynamic motion that inspired artists in succeeding generations and cultures, from ancient Rome to the European Renaissance and the United States in the eighteenth and nineteenth centuries.

People in the ancient Americas established their own sculptural traditions, including Mayan temples and jade ornaments, as well as Aztec monuments depicting feathered serpents and divine eagles. The Inca (or Inka) built thousands of miles of roads through some of the world's most mountainous lands and created stone buildings on high mountain peaks, like Machu Picchu, that are in fact works of art and have withstood earthquakes for hundreds of years.

Asian artisans created some of the most intricate, detailed, and astonishing sculpture and architectural achievements the world has ever seen. China's Qin emperor was buried in a tomb with thousands of life-sized terra-cotta soldiers, each one unique and different from the soldier beside him. The World Heritage site of Angkor Wat in Cambodia has served as both a Hindu and a Buddhist temple in its long history and includes miles of detailed carvings depicting religious scenes and teachings.

Many sculptural traditions in Africa are lost to history because of colonial upheavals and tropical weather that quickly destroyed any wood or fiber sculptures that were made. Surviving stone and metal sculptures include the stunning Benin bronzes and detailed Ife sculpture heads.

Polynesians created some of the most evocative and unique works of sculpture ever seen, including the Tiki and unforgettable Easter Island ancestor statues, the giant *moai*. Australia's indigenous people, the Aboriginals, created vast areas of petroglyphs and rock art, including over 1 million images in the protected area of Murujuga.

First Nations people in North America did not just create the cliff dwellings of Mesa Verde a thousand years ago, but more recently, Hopi kachina. The Fort Ancient culture created the Great Serpent Mound in Ohio, a massive outdoor land sculpture that, hundreds of years later, in 1970, inspired the land artist Robert Smithson to build the *Spiral Jetty* on the shores of the Great Salt Lake in Utah.

Historically, much sculpture was created for religious purposes. Some of the greatest sculptures were created to inspire religious believers, from Michelangelo's *Pietà* to India's Ajanta Caves and Indonesia's sleeping Buddha statues. Some of the earliest known sculptures, the Venus figurines found in Europe's Neolithic caves, are believed to be statues of fertility goddesses. Both the Greeks and Romans erected marble and bronze statues of gods and goddesses from Zeus to Aphrodite, the goddess of love.

The way people have seen the sculpture of the past has not always been the way it was viewed by the people who created it. One of the biggest changes in art history came when modern science uncovered the true appearance of ancient Greek and Roman marble statues. Although Italian Renaissance artists like Leonardo da Vinci thought that paint should stay on canvases and marble should remain pure white, ancient people carved their statues from white stone, which was then painted in a rainbow of brilliant colors, ornamented in gold, and finished with precious stones to create flashing, glittering eyes. Even the giant ancestor statues, the *moai* of Easter Island, had eyes made of white coral and red or black colored stone.

Sculpture differs from two-dimensional art like painting or drawing because it is usually meant to be seen from all sides. The friezes on the Parthenon atop the ancient Acropolis in Athens were more than 30 feet (9.1 m) high. Only the front of the mythological figures carved by the Athenian sculptor Phidias could be seen from the ground, but even the feet of the gods and horses, as well as their backs, were completely painted, in case someone could catch a glimpse.

Today, sculpture is no longer restricted to public places, created to honor rulers and impress conquered vassals, or used for religious purposes. Sculpture can be personal and decorative and created purely for visual enjoyment. Contemporary sculptors around the world are rediscovering the cultural heritage of their nations as well as creating new art forms. Like Alexander Calder, the American sculptor who invented the mobile in the twentieth century, today's sculptors on all continents are working in every type of material imaginable, from an artist who creates new sculpture out of old skateboard decks to a mixed media and fashion expert who immerses gallery viewers in an underwater world made of crocheted coral and fish.

KEY TERMS

Abstract: Art, including sculpture, that depicts shapes and forms that are not easily recognized as people, animals, or natural objects.

Alabaster: A type of white gypsum that is partially transparent when carved and polished.

Armature: A framework that supports a clay sculpture while it is being created.

Assemblage: A type of sculpture made from different objects assembled into a new whole.

Bas-relief: A type of low relief in which figures are raised only slightly from the underlying stone or metal.

Brass: A gold-colored metal alloy made from copper and zinc.

Bronze: A brownish metal alloy made from a mixture of copper and tin.

Bust: A sculpture representing a human head and shoulders.

Carving: The oldest sculptural technique, in which material is removed from a basic shape using tools.

Casting: A method of creating multiple sculptures by pouring material (plaster, molten metal, plastic, glass) into a mold.

Chisel: A metal carving tool used for wood or stone carving.

Figurative: A type of art that depicts a recognizable person, animal, or object from the natural world.

Firing: The process of heating clay to produce a durable, hard final product.

Frieze: A horizontal area of decoration on buildings, including Greek or Roman temples.

Glazing: A ceramic material that can be painted on clay and used in the firing process.

Lost-wax method: The method of using a wax cast to create a finished metal product.

Mobile: A sculpture with moving parts, pioneered by the twentieth-century artist Alexander Calder.

Modeling: The technique of adding material like clay onto a base form to create a sculpture.

Mold: The reverse impression of a sculpture that can be used to create copies through casting.

Monument: A building and sculptural element created to draw attention to or memorialize a person, religious entity, or event.

Patina: A protective, colored coating created naturally or deliberately by artists on bronze, copper, or iron sculptures.

Plaster cast: A plaster copy of a sculpture that is usually used to create a mold for metal sculpture casting.

Plinth: The base of a sculpture.

Relief: A type of sculpture in metal or stone in which figures are partially raised above the background.

Terra-cotta: A type of reddish pottery that can be fired at lower temperatures than other ceramics.

Whiteware: A kind of white clay pottery often found in South America and Asia.

CHAPTER 1 AFRICA

Africa is considered the birthplace of humanity, but some of the history of African sculpture is buried under desert sands. We lack some historical knowledge of African sculpture made of wood or clay, because such sculptures couldn't survive rainy forest conditions for very long. From the art that has survived, it is clear that African sculpture is among the most diverse of the world's sculptural traditions, from West African expressive art to the monuments and sculpture of Nubian kings and the artwork of Great Zimbabwe.

THE NUBIAN KINGS OF KUSH: GLIMPSES OF ROYAL SPLENDOR

The history of the Nubian kings and the ancient Kingdom of Kush is intertwined with ancient Egypt. Much of Kush's sculpture and monuments have been hidden through history and have been revealed only with twentieth- and twenty-first-century archaeological discoveries, which are ongoing. The Kingdom of Kush in northeastern Africa is centered along the Nile River. Civilization in this region dates back before 3300 BCE.

Egypt and Kush were always linked in art and trade. In 744 BCE, Egypt was conquered by the Kushite King Piye, who became the first pharaoh of Egypt's 25th dynasty. Piye's son Taharqa built vast monuments in Egypt and Kush. Rulers of the 25th dynasty are called the Black Pharaohs.

Some of the sculptures from the Kingdom of Kush that are known today were excavated in the twentieth- and twenty-first century by Charles Bonnet, a Swiss archaeologist. Bonnet recognized that Kush had its own artistic and cultural tradition, distinct from those of Egypt. As one example, Nubian kings built pyramids, but these pyramids were tall and slender, not triangular like Egyptian pyramids.

This statue of King Taharqa worshipping the falcon god Hemen can be viewed in the Louvre in Paris.

Images of King Taharqa, one of the most powerful 25th dynasty rulers of Egypt and Nubia, show a pair of realistic cobras and African-appearing features. One beautiful statue, which is exhibited in the Louvre in Paris, shows Taharqa worshipping the falcon god Hemen in a blending of African and Egyptian artistic influences.

Five striking dark granite statues of the pharaohs of the 25th dynasty were uncovered in Kerma in 2011 and are exhibited in the Kerma museum. The statues have African features and were deliberately broken by succeeding pharaohs to eliminate public knowledge of the powerful 25th dynasty kings who ruled Egypt for almost 100 years.

Nubian kings were powerful, but so were Nubian queens. Historical records refer to Nubian queens called "Candace," or "Kandake." The word means "sister," and there were many Candaces in ancient Kush. One famous sandstone relief from the funeral chapel of Queen Shanakdakhete, the first Kushite queen to rule on her own, is exhibited in the British Museum in London. Other sculptures of Queen Shanakdakhete have been discovered, showing that she ruled Nubia between 170 and 150 BCE.

This relief of Queen Shanakdakhete can be found in the British Museum.

BENIN BRONZE ARTISTS AND LOST-WAX CASTING

Today there is a West African nation of Benin, but the medieval Benin Kingdom of the Edo people, the creators of the famous Benin bronzes, was in what is now the neighboring country of Nigeria.

Benin's bronzes are varied in size, subject matter, and artistic styles. The bronzes are not even made exclusively of bronze, which is an alloy, or mixture, of copper and tin. Some are made from brass, an alloy of copper and zinc. The plaques and sculptures adorned the walls of the ruler, or Oba of Benin. The Benin Kingdom lasted from the fourteenth to the nineteenth century.

In 1897 a British expedition traveled to the Kingdom of Benin. Although the expedition was warned not to try to enter Benin's royal city while ceremonies were under way, the group continued and was attacked by royal warriors, with only two Europeans surviving the conflict.

In retaliation, Europeans invaded the city, destroying the palace and seizing artwork, including sculptures of kings, queens, African wildlife, and high-relief plaques. More than 2,400 of the Benin bronzes were transported away from Africa. Today, only about 50 of the sculptures remain in Africa; the majority are in European and American art collections.

Most of the bronze plaques are done in the style of high relief,

A Benin bronze of Benin warriors.

which means the image extends more than half of its height away from the background. Freestanding molded heads of warriors, kings, and queens show a wide range of realistic and stylized appearances, as well as bronze polished surfaces with a patina (coating) ranging from dark black to gold and brass. Expressively modeled animal sculptures include lions, leopards, birds, and fish. Benin bronzes are very detailed, whether they are stylized, abstract, or realistic depictions of people and animals. The details were enabled by the Benin artists' use of the "lost-wax" metal casting technique, which enabled them to model and cast thinner plaques than European artists of the same time period. The artists belonged to a special guild and lived in their own compound, exclusively devoted to creating sculpture.

A bronze head of Queen Idia.

Melted Wax Creates Intricate Bronze Sculptures

Lost-wax sculptures have been discovered dating as far back as 5,000 years ago. In the simplest type of lost-wax sculpture, a model is made of wax, and a network of wax pipes called "sprues" are added, which allow hot metal to flow evenly and the melted wax to escape. The wax model is covered with a plaster cast. When the outer plaster cast has hardened, hot metal is poured in. The wax melts and escapes. When the metal is cooled, the mold is broken or removed, leaving a metal duplicate of the original wax sculpture. Smaller lost-wax sculptures can be cast in one piece. Larger ones are usually cast in multiple sections and joined together.

AFRICAN MASKS: SPIRITUAL POWER AND CULTURAL HISTORY

Masks have been made and used throughout African history, but they are primarily associated with West, Central, and southern Africa. The kinds of masks made in Africa are as diverse as Africa's many people, but masks can be categorized into four major types: spirit or religious masks, ancestor masks, portraits of leaders and rulers, and symbols of power.

Burkina Faso, located in West Africa, is one of the African nations best known for its masks. The masks created by the Bwa and Nuna people in Burkina Faso illustrate nature spirits, including buffalo, hawk, crocodile, and flying spirits. The masks, made from wood and natural fiber, are highly stylized and patterned. Each year, thousands of people visit Dédougou in Burkina Faso to watch Festima, a festival that keeps traditional mask culture alive. Festima features local masked dancers and others from Benin, Togo, Côte d'Ivoire (Ivory Coast), Senegal, and Mali.

Other mask traditions celebrate beauty. The Punu people in Gabon create white-faced feminine masks with delicate features that illustrate the spirit

A man wears a traditional Burkina Faso mask.

world. Dogon people from Mali create many different carved-wood masks representing ancestors or spirits. Some masks feature combinations of wood and raffia (a type of fiber) that create dramatic effects, including very large raffia "coiffures" that cover the whole head or shoulders.

Some masks are made of fabric, shells, beads, or animal skin. A mask depicting an ancestral, powerful king from the Kuba Kingdom in the Democratic Republic of the Congo features leopard skin and cowrie shells. Cowrie shells are valuable in the Congo, which has only a small area of coastline on the Atlantic Ocean. Masks with exaggerated, stylized features are often carved from a single piece of wood to indicate spiritual power in many cultural traditions, from Congo to Cameroon.

Masked Dogon dancers take part in a ritual.

Masks that combine the power of natural elements and animals are also used in ceremonies and dances. Helmet masks cover the face and head and may extend over the entire upper body. For example, a *pumbu* mask worn by the Eastern Pende people in Congo covers the upper body and expresses courage and anger through its white-rimmed eyes and diamond-shaped pattern, representing royal kingship.

IFE PORTRAIT HEADS

The city of Ife in Nigeria has been a center of Yoruba culture since the tenth century CE. A German anthropologist visited the city in the early twentieth century and brought realistic, beautiful terra-cotta clay sculpture heads back to Europe. European scholars mistakenly concluded that the realistic and balanced sculptures of men's and women's heads were the result of influence from ancient Greece or Rome.

Following the initial discovery, many stone, copper, brass, and terra-cotta Ife sculpture heads have been uncovered, showing a 500-year tradition of sculpture created by Yoruba people between about 900 and 1400 CE. Naturalistic and realistic copper alloy masks and heads have been found that represent rulers and deities of the Yoruba people. Most of the Ife heads were made using the lost-wax technique or terra-cotta clay formed by hand modeling. The Ife heads are now used to represent several cultural events, organizations, and businesses in Nigeria, and they have taken on cultural significance worldwide for people of Nigerian heritage and ancestry.

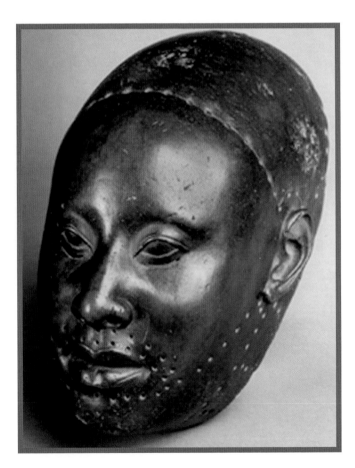

A Yoruba copper mask for King Obalufon.

IVORY SCULPTURE IS NO LONGER LEGAL

When African people began carving sculptures out of elephant ivory, elephants were not endangered or threatened animals. It has been illegal to import elephant ivory into the United States since 1990, and no commercial use of elephant ivory is permitted.

Ivory sculptures began to be made after 1490 in Africa, influenced by the arrival of Europeans into Nigeria, Congo, and Sierra Leone. Antique ivory sculptures from the age of exploration were sometimes carved with European-inspired scenes and features. Ivory masks and scepters were sometimes carved for African and European kings.

Starting in the eighteenth century, some elephant tusks were carved into elaborate scenes of triumph and animal hunts. The tusks were called "olifants" and could be blown like horns, signaling to hunters or to announce a battle.

An olifant made of elephant ivory.

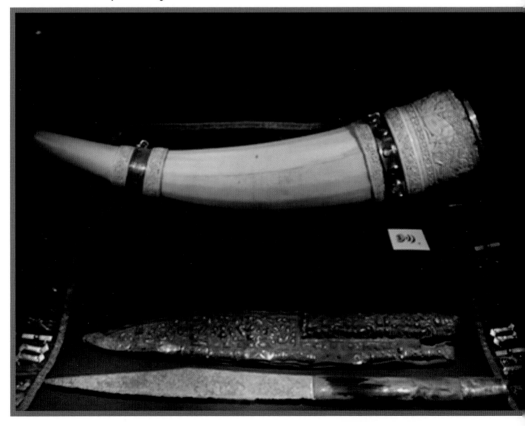

GREAT ZIMBABWE'S SOAPSTONE BIRDS

Great Zimbabwe comprises a group of ruins of a powerful city and kingdom in southern Africa, built between the eleventh and fifteenth centuries. Great Zimbabwe was the capital of the Queen of Sheba and the main city of the Bantu civilization of Shona people. The curved stone walls of Great Zimbabwe seem to blend into the natural landscape with ease.

When explorers reached Great Zimbabwe's ruins in the nineteenth century, they found stone pillars around a central altar. Each of the pillars was topped by a realistic soapstone bird sculpture. The birds are thought to represent sacred, spiritually powerful eagles. By the time more explorers arrived, the birds and pedestals had been damaged, and only six large and two small birds were left. The birds' realistic style and powerful imagery was incorrectly attributed to non-African artists by colonial explorers. Today, the Zimbabwean origin of the birds is recognized, and the birds are used on Zimbabwe's flag, money, and other state symbols.

The Great Zimbabwe stone ruins.

THE EXAGGERATED FIGURES OF NOK TERRA-COTTAS

The Nok people lived in West Africa in what is today part of Niger and Nigeria. Between 500 BCE and the first century CE, they created terra-cotta sculptures ranging from small pendants to life-sized human and animal images. Nok figures of humans often have detailed hairstyles and wear elaborate jewelry. Their bodies may be elongated or stylized, but facial features are realistic, if sometimes exaggerated. Some art historians have wondered if some of the Nok terra-cotta figures represent forms of illness and could be meant to ward off sickness or encourage a cure, because some of the figures have enlarged arms and legs or paralyzed facial features.

A Nok terra-cotta sculpture on display at the Louvre.

NNENNA OKORE: INSPIRED BY THE ENVIRONMENT AND NATURE

Nnenna Okore's installation Lifeforce.

Nnenna Okore is a contemporary Nigerian artist who creates large abstract sculpture and art installations out of natural substances, including ceramic, fiber, and paper. Nnenna's work has been exhibited worldwide, and she is a professor of art and chair of the Art Department at Chicago's North Park University. Her art uses primarily natural earth tones and colors and represents the earth's vulnerability and environmental devastation. She also seeks to portray the sublimity of nature and show how transient human labor is in the face of the power of nature.

GONÇALO MABUNDA: SCULPTURES OUT OF WEAPONS

This piece from Gonçalo Mabunda is made from armaments and ammunition from Mozambique during its civil war.

Gonçalo Mabunda is a sculptor from Mozambique in East Africa who has exhibited his artwork in galleries around the world, including Paris, New York, South Korea, London, and Tokyo. Gonçalo creates masks, standing sculptures, and furniture out of recycled weapons, including shell casings and guns. Although Gonçalo's art echoes traditional African culture, his colors and approach reflect contemporary culture, with bright colors and textures. Gonçalo transforms ugly instruments of war into beautiful and whimsical objects. He was inspired to create his sculptures to heal his country, which endured a long and violent civil war.

In 2013, an El Anatsui installation covered the façade of the Royal Academy of Arts in London.

EL ANATSUI: ART OUT OF FOUND OBJECTS

Born in Ghana in 1944, El Anatsui is a sculptor who makes flexible sculptures that can be changed in form and altered wherever where they are displayed. El Anatsui uses clay and metal and has become famous for creating large structures out of metal bottle caps. He is considered an abstract, not figurative, artist, although his assemblages of discarded materials comments on how everyday objects can become works of art. His work has been shown in galleries around the world and is included in collections in the Metropolitan Museum of Art, Los Angeles County Museum of Art, the British Museum in London, and the Pompidou Centre in Paris.

CHAPTER  ASIA

From the earliest stone monuments discovered in ancient Turkey to the Ajanta Caves in India and the giant Tian Tan Buddha, Asian artists have been creating sculpture for more than 10,000 years. Asian sculptural traditions often portray religious or cultural figures, from the Buddha to Hindu deities. Contemporary Asian sculptures experiment with materials and subjects on an international stage.

CHINA'S ANCIENT TERRA-COTTA ARMY

Over 2,000 years ago, from 246 to 210 BCE, China's first emperor, Qin Shi Huang, fought battles to unite warring Chinese provinces. In 221 BCE, Qin defeated the last independent Chinese province to become China's first Qin Emperor. At this time, realistic sculptures were being made in ancient Greece and Rome, and major monuments were being built, but none larger than Qin's tomb, and none had so many detailed sculptures as Qin's Terra-Cotta Army.

Qin is regarded as a great military and cultural leader, but he was also known for his brutal methods of executing rivals. When the emperor was a young adult, his biological father, Lu, organized a rebellion against him. Qin stopped the rebellion, but more assassination attempts followed, and Qin became increasingly fearful of death. In case he could not live forever, Qin began building a replica of his earthly capital.

Qin's terra-cotta army uncovered in the tomb.

In addition to Qin's terra-cotta army, sculptures of their horses were excavated, too.

The tomb lay undisturbed until 1974, when farmers discovered the first of more than 8,000 terra-cotta soldiers in Lintong District in Xi'an, the capital of Shaanxi Province in Central China. The emperor's terra-cotta soldiers were the first statues discovered in the burial monument, which covers 38 square miles (98 sq km).

In addition to soldiers, terra-cotta replicas of many members of Qin's court have been found in the monument, including musicians, dancers, and court officials. Terra-cotta horses and bronze chariots have also been uncovered.

Terra-cotta is a type of red or brown clay pottery that undergoes firing in a kiln at a low temperature. The statues were cast in a basic mold, and artisans added details to individualize each statue before firing, so that each soldier is unique. The artisans painted the army in bright colors, including a type of artificial purple found only in ancient China. However, the colors are faded today because the soldiers were not painted and glazed before firing. An estimated 700,000 Chinese artisans and workers created the thousands of sculptures found in Qin's tomb.

CAMBODIA'S MAGICAL STONE CITY

Angkor Wat (*wat* means "temple" in Cambodian) is the most famous of more than 100 temples that were built by the Khmer civilization 1,000 years ago in northern Cambodia. The massive Angkor complex was built primarily of sandstone, with sculptures added over six centuries. The temples were originally dedicated to Vishnu, a Hindu god, by the Khmer King Suryavarman II. When the complex was first built, it was also the capital of the king's empire.

When the Thai people conquered the Khmer Empire in Cambodia in 1431, the temples were converted to Buddhism, so monuments and sculptures at Angkor Wat now reflect both Hindu and Buddhist beliefs. Angkor Wat's temples are surrounded by a moat that reflects the central tower, creating an impression of beauty and serenity.

The temples and walls at Angkor Wat are a World Heritage site and represent a stunning achievement of architecture and stone sculpture. The temples each contain a gallery (hall or corridor) that is lined with columns and bas-relief

The Angkor complex in Cambodia.

Churning of the Sea of Milk is one of the best known bas-relief sculptures on Angkor Wat's walls.

friezes. A frieze is a long section of wall located above columns but below a roof or ceiling.

Many of the inner friezes depict scenes from two Hindu epics, the Mahabharata and the Ramayana. The best known bas-relief sculpture on Angkor Wat's walls is the Churning of the Sea of Milk. The sculpture shows the Hindu god Vishnu and over 100 other gods and divine creatures. Vishnu is depicted in god and turtle form on the frieze. Angkor Wat's friezes extend for miles, and nearly every surface is carved. Mythical creatures include unicorns, dragons, griffins, *nagas* (a half-human, half-cobra figure) and divine, magical dancing cloud and air spirits called *apsaras*.

More Stone Than All of Egypt's Pyramids

Angkor Wat contains more stone than all the Egyptian pyramids combined. Skilled craftsmen carved miles of reliefs depicting every imaginable mythical creature, as well as illustrated scenes from Hindu and Buddhist teachings. Angkor Wat's stone towers are "temple mountains" that represent Mount Meru, one of the tallest mountains in the Himalayas. Most sculptures on Angkor Wat's temple walls are bas-reliefs. A bas-relief differs from a freestanding statue; it is a type of sculpture where the figures are raised above a flat stone or clay background. The human forms or other elements remain attached to the solid base of clay or stone.

INDIA'S DANCING SCULPTURES

The earliest sculptures in India date back to one of the world's first cities in the Indus Valley. A famous bronze sculpture of a dancing girl that is more 4,500 years old was discovered in the ancient city of Mohenjo-daro, located in modern-day Pakistan.

Dancing Girl from the ancient city of Mohenjo-daro.

The theme of dancing appears throughout the history of Indian sculpture, particularly in images that depict Hindu gods. Some of the most famous Indian sculptures are bronze images of a dancing Shiva, depicting the four-armed god dancing inside a flaming halo in his roles as world creator, preserver, and destroyer.

Indian artisans created caves filled with religious sculptures. Among the most beautiful are the dancing princesses, nature spirits, and nymphs depicted on the walls of the Ajanta Caves, a complex of 29 caves first built in the fourth century CE. The caves contain bas-reliefs and paintings. The largest and most extensive of many Indian religious caves are the Ellora Caves, carved between 350 and 700 CE. Their sculptures depict images from the Hindu, Buddhist, and Jain faiths. The largest monument at the Ellora Caves is the Kailasa Temple, which is intended to depict Shiva's home in the Himalayas. The Kailasa Temple is the world's largest monument carved out of a single block of stone.

Not all Indian sculpture depicts dancing gods or religious figures. The Taj Mahal has no sculptures of people or gods. It is one of the world's most famous structures and is built of white marble. It was constructed by the Mughal Emperor Shah Jahan in memory of his wife, Mumtaz Mahal. Its domes and spires echo natural shapes, including lotus flowers and the onion. The Mughal emperors were Muslim, a religion that uses calligraphy and patterns as art, so all carvings in the Taj Mahal are patterns or writing, not statues of dancers or Hindu gods and goddesses.

The Taj Mahal in India was constructed entirely of white marble.

THE SANXINGDUI DISCOVERY

Boldly sculpted bronze heads, ancient carved jades, and gold and bronze masks, 1,000 years older than the Qin Emperor's terra-cotta army, were discovered in 1986 in Sichuan Province in southwestern China. The Sanxingdui artifacts were made by artists from the ancient Chinese kingdom of Shu during the twelfth and eleventh centuries BCE, and their discovery has rewritten Chinese art and cultural history, offering a contrast to other early Chinese art and culture from central China, which was thought to be the only ancient Chinese cultural center, located 750 miles to the east.

The bronze heads found in Sichuan Province are sculpted in an impressionistic and exaggerated style that is completely different from other Chinese and world art. Animal-faced sculptures, a life-sized priest with bold almond-shaped eyes, and a sacrificial altar exemplify the Sanxingdui culture's unique artistic vision.

Sanxingdui people had strong metal-working skills. A large, freestanding bronze tree depicts magical branches, leaves, and animals. Dozens of human bronze masks are molded with exaggerated features and large almond-shaped or protruding eyes. Other masks depict mythical animals, eagles, or other birds.

An ancient bronze mask found in the Sichuan Province.

CHINA BOASTS THE WORLD'S LARGEST BUDDHA SCULPTURES

China is home to the largest sculptures in the world, and they all depict the Buddha. The Leshan Giant Buddha was carved out of red sandstone in Sichuan Province between 713 and 803 CE. At 233 feet (71 m), as tall as a 21-story building, the Giant Buddha is the tallest stone sculpture ever created. An adult person can sit on its smallest toenail. In 2002, the Spring Temple Buddha was completed. It stands more than 393 feet (120 m) high and is made of 1,100 pieces of copper that weigh more than 1,000 tons.

Buddhism was introduced to China from India in the second century BCE but became more popular 400 years later during the second century CE. The earliest sculptures weren't of the Buddha himself, but of the Bodhi tree under which the Buddha received enlightenment, or of an empty seat or footprint. These sculptures evolved into Chinese pagodas, the tiered towers whose form is familiar worldwide.

Chinese artists carved reliefs in rock caves that illustrated Buddhist teachings and the Buddha himself. Dozens of famous caves or cave complexes have been excavated and preserved. The Mogao Caves include more than 2,400 clay sculptures. From bas-reliefs to massive Buddhas, the Mogao Caves also hold the Maitreya Buddha, which is 116 feet (35.5 m) tall. The Maitreya Buddha was built by China's Empress Wu Zetian, who oversaw construction of these and many other caves in the seventh century CE.

Other Chinese Buddhist sculptures depict enlightened followers of the Buddha, or *bodhisattvas*. Many Chinese *bodhisattvas* are female, including Guan Yin. Other sculptures, meanwhile, are of massive Temple guardians called Nio.

The Leshan Giant Buddha is the tallest sculpture ever created.

JAPANESE SCULPTURE: 15,000 YEARS IN THE MAKING

Although most traditional Japanese sculptures depict Buddha or Buddhist teachings, the styles differ from Chinese or Indian Buddhist art. Japan's Nara period, from 646 to 794 CE, was considered the Golden Age of Japanese sculpture and combined influences from Chinese, Indian, and Persian art to create a uniquely Japanese style.

Traditional Japanese sculpture began nearly 15,000 years earlier. These early sculptures, made from ceramics or metal, reflected the Jōmon culture, which dominated Japan for thousands of years, beginning in 14,000 BCE. Early Jōmon sculpture include Dogū, which are small human and animal figures with exaggerated eyes and stylized bodies. Jōmon culture lasted until 200 years before the current era as other Japanese culture also evolved.

When the Nara period began, *busshi*, the Japanese word for sculptors, were inspired by Chinese and Indian art. They soon began to create their own style, however, and introduced bronze, clay, and lacquered wood to their sculptures. A painted clay Shitsukongō-shin (temple protector) shows a fierce and warlike Nio, a temple guardian meant to encourage people to follow Buddha's teachings. Over time, Japanese *busshi* created many fiery images of demons to protect Japanese temples, and realistic, expressive *devas* (followers of Buddha) showing diverse emotions.

The Nara Period also included the creation of the largest bronze statue in the world, located at the Tōshōdai-ji Temple. Nara Daibutsu, completed in 752 CE, is the most famous Buddha sculpture of Japan's Nara Period: it is 49 feet (15 m) tall.

A Dogū figurine.

CHINESE JADE: MORE VALUABLE THAN GOLD OR DIAMONDS

A Chinese jade teapot.

Chinese people have carved jade into useful or decorative shapes since the Stone Age. Early jade carvings date to 4000 BCE. For the Chinese, jade has a spiritual, emotional, and cultural value far greater than gold or diamonds. And the sophistication of the carvings increased with every generation of artists. Jade is so highly prized that through much of Chinese history, it was reserved for royalty. Today, jade carvings and sculptures are enjoyed by all Chinese and sold around the world.

In addition to its use in jewelry and decorative objects, jade has a long history of use in clothing—both for the living and for the dead. Royalty and nobility were traditionally laid to rest wearing suits of jade beads. Two of the most famous jade burial suits consisted of more than 2,000 jade plaques sewn together with gold thread, belonging to Prince Liu Sheng and his wife, Princess Dou Wan, who ruled Zhongshan between 154 and 113 BCE, during the Han Dynasty.

Greetingman in Seoul, South Korea.

KOREAN SCULPTORS: BRINGING ART TO PUBLIC SPACES

The 2018 Winter Olympics in Pyeongchang, South Korea, drew the world's attention to some of Korea's contemporary artists. One of them, Yoo Young-ho, is a South Korean artist whose *Greetingman Project* features a large male sculpture bowing to visitors in Seoul, South Korea. Yoo's work encourages friendship and world peace and has been installed in public spaces around the world. It's also featured in Marvel's Avengers movies.

Kim Yongwon is another South Korean sculptor who creates large-scale works for display in public spaces, including Dondaemun History & Culture Park in Seoul. Kim's sculpture *Shadow of a Shadow* is a 26-foot-tall (8 m) bronze human figure that depicts different parts of a personality arising from a single person.

JAPAN'S SKATEBOARD SCULPTOR

A Haroshi exhibit in London.

The Japanese sculptor and artist Haroshi has no formal art education, but he has become famous for his blending of youth culture and fine art. Haroshi has exhibited his fascinating sculptures, made from used skateboard decks, all over the world. His exhibitions in world cities like New York and Paris have titles that echo skateboarding culture, such as "Skate and Destroy." Haroshi has made trophies shaped like Nike shoes, monuments to Skateboarders' Unity, and a realistic polished broken heart called *Life with Pain*. His large sculpture *A Vulture Waits for the Dead* is made of hundreds of used skateboard decks. For this work, Haroshi cut up and recombined some of the decks, and left others whole to form the vulture's wings and other parts of the sculpture.

ELEVATING GRAFFITI TO THE HIGHEST LEVEL

One of DALeast's pieces in Berlin.

The Chinese artist DALeast is referred to as a "street artist," but his urban art pushes the limits of the possible and even the probable. DALeast has worked on projects around the world since 2005. His solo art exhibitions have been held in New York, London, Milan, and Melbourne, Australia. DALeast uses paint and metal to create astonishing images of animals and nature in action on walls, buildings, and abandoned spaces around the world. Some of his most surprising work includes a massive eagle in flight in Boras, Sweden; the Antenna Garden in Melbourne; and the DALeast London Dare, a live street-art project the artist conducted over one week in London in 2013.

CHAPTER ❸ EUROPE

Europe is home to the oldest sculpture ever discovered, the Lion-Man of the Hohlenstein-Stadel, found in a German cave in 1939. The Lion-Man is 40,000 years old and was carved out of mammoth ivory. Over the centuries, sculpture in Europe continued to change to include Classical Greek and Roman statues celebrating the human body, and Italian Renaissance sculptors of the human spirit like Michelangelo. By the time of Michelangelo, the classic sculptures of Ancient Greece and Rome had faded to pure white marble. But the glittering white stone held a secret that science has revealed: when they were first made, the white stone was painted in bright, vivid colors.

GREEK SCULPTURE: CAPTURING THE BODY IN MOTION

Art historians classify Ancient Greek sculpture into four periods: the Geometric, Archaic, Classical, and Hellenistic. The Geometric period began about 1000 BCE and lasted approximately 300 years. Early Geometric period statues were often carved from ivory or cast in bronze, including a series of ivory statues of goddesses found in the Dipylon graves (Kerameikos).

Experts in Ancient Greek art have suggested that the Greek sculptors of the Archaic period (approximately 700–500 BCE) were influenced by Ancient Egyptian artists. Many Archaic Greek statues depict young men (*kouros*) and women (*kore*) in a ritual standing pose with their left foot forward, like Egyptian monuments.

The change from Archaic sculptures to Classical Greek sculpture occurred over at least 100 years, between 500 and 400 BCE. Carved figures found at the Acropolis in Athens include the Kritios Boy, a marble sculpture that is much more naturalistic than previous Greek *kouros* statues. Artemesion Zeus/Poseidon is a dramatic, 6.5-foot-tall (2 m) bronze found in a shipwreck off Cape Artemision in 1928.

The Parthenon sculptures are some of the most notable pieces of Greek artwork.

Starting around 450 BCE, Classical Greek sculptors created some of the most famous statues of all time, including images of the goddess Nike, the Parthenon sculptures, and the Capitoline Venus. We know many of these sculptures today because of Roman copies and the writings of Roman historians, such as Pliny the Elder. Famous Greek sculptors include Praxiteles, Phidias, Myron, and Lysippus, who was Alexander the Great's official sculptor. Classical Greek sculptures represent idealized bodies, faces, and poses, in contrast with the later Hellenistic art, which included all ages, types of subjects, and poses.

The Hellenistic period dates from approximately 323 to 146 BCE and includes some of the most dramatic sculptures made by Greek culture. Hellenistic sculpture captured action and personality, as seen in sculptures like Laocoön and His Sons, depicting the legend of a Trojan family fighting deadly snakes. A bronze called *Boxer at Rest* by Apollonius shows a realistically scarred, defeated athlete.

Boxer at Rest *on display in Rome.*

ROMAN ART: INSPIRATION FROM MANY LANDS

Roman history begins with its legendary founding in 753 BCE on the banks of the Tiber River by Romulus, Rome's first recorded king. Early Roman sculpture was inspired by the Etruscans, the culture that preceded the Romans in Italy. Etruscan sculpture has elements of Greek and Egyptian stylization as well as a uniquely Etruscan interest in marriage, love, and family. One beautiful example includes the Sarcophagus of the Spouses, a life-sized-terra-cotta burial sculpture created around 520 BCE.

According to legend, the Roman Republic began in 509 BCE when the Etruscan King Tarquinius was overthrown. The Republican period of Roman sculpture (509–27 BCE) is marked by realism. Art historians call the style "veristic," and it includes every flaw a subject might have, from wrinkles to bald heads and large, bumpy noses.

The Sarcophagus of the Spouses terra-cotta burial sculpture.

When Augustus became the first Roman emperor in 27 BCE, Roman sculpture entered the Imperial Period, which lasted for more than 300 years. Sculptural styles between 27 BCE and 337 CE are named after the primary emperor during each period, from the initial Augustan style to the era of Constantine, the first Christian emperor who ruled from 307 to 337 CE. The sculpture Augustus of Prima Porta shows the first emperor as an idealized Greek-inspired god wearing Roman armor. A bearded bust of the emperor Hadrian, who ruled from 117 to 138 CE, shows his interest in Greek culture through his Greek beard combined with Roman realism.

Romans created a nearly infinite variety of monuments, from arches commemorating triumphs in battle chiseled from marble

Augustus of Prima Porta.

to bronze statues of gods, goddesses, and emperors. At its greatest extent in the third century CE, the Roman Empire stretched from Spain, North Africa, and Great Britain to present-day Turkey, Iran, and Iraq. From massive columns and monuments decorated with carved marble friezes to portrait busts that depicted the faces of Romans as they appeared in life, Roman art took inspiration from the lands and cultures the Romans conquered, from Ancient Greece to the Middle East.

RENAISSANCE SCULPTORS: CLASSICAL INSPIRATION LEADS TO GREATNESS

In art history, the "Renaissance" refers to a rebirth or "reboot" of the art and culture of Ancient Greece and Rome that took place in Europe during the fourteenth through the sixteenth centuries. The best known Renaissance sculptors came from Italy, but Renaissance sculpture was created throughout all parts of Europe

Donatello's David *is a must-see when visiting Florence.*

between about 1350 and 1610. The European Renaissance is one of the first historical periods where artists' names were widely known, like Michelangelo, as were the names of the wealthy patrons who paid for their creations, like the Medici, the ruling family of Florence.

The Early Renaissance sculptor Donatello created two versions of the biblical hero David that featured dynamic poses. Donatello's bronze *David*, completed in 1440, is the first fully nude, freestanding bronze male sculpture made in Europe since the days of ancient Rome. The slightly less-than-life-sized bronze features a young, slim hero standing on Goliath's head in a relaxed pose typical of the Renaissance called *contrapposto*.

The "High Renaissance" refers to the period of Italian art that began with Leonardo da Vinci's painting *The Last Supper* in Milan in the 1490s. It continued to 1527, when Rome was sacked by Charles V., the Holy Roman Emperor and King of Italy. Michelangelo Buonarroti was a native of Florence and created his greatest sculptures for the Medici family and the Roman Catholic Church. Michelangelo's *Pietà* in St. Peter's Basilica in Rome was completed in 1499; it depicts a young Mary holding the crucified Christ on her lap. The artist's *David*, completed in 1504, is a 17-foot-tall (5.1 m) freestanding marble sculpture representing the freedom of the Republic of Florence and the power of the Medici family.

The Renaissance was not limited to Italy. Artists created sculptures expressing movement and human emotion throughout Europe during the fifteenth and sixteenth centuries. In 1410 the Dutch sculptors Claus Sluter and Claus de Werve chiseled a series of realistic, praying and grieving alabaster mourners for the tomb of Philip the Bold, Duke of Burgundy. The Flemish artist Giambologna created some of the best known late Renaissance sculptures, including the *Rape of the Sabine Women* and *Hercules and the Centaur Nessus*.

Flemish artist Giambolona's Hercules and the Centaur Nessus.

Greek and Roman Statues: White Marble or Painted?

One of the greatest misunderstandings in art history occurred during the Italian Renaissance, when ancient Greek and Roman statues were uncovered after being buried for hundreds of years. Michelangelo, along with other Renaissance sculptors, believed that these ancient treasures had always been pure white, unaware that time and weather had removed their original painted colors.

To Renaissance artists, white was considered a sign of purity, and bare marble signified artistic taste and even intelligence. Painting and sculpture were pitted against each other in some Renaissance debates: Leonardo da Vinci, among others, believed that "paint had no place on marble." Recent optical techniques and testing have uncovered the truth: Classical marble and bronze statues were painted in bright colors, from realistic skin tones to rainbow clothing, shining armor, and deep layers of glazing or gold leaf for jewelry.

PREHISTORIC SCULPTURE

The oldest known sculpture, the Lion-Man of Hohlenstein-Stadel, was discovered in a cave in Germany in 1939. The Lion-Man is approximately 40,000 years old and is a 12.2-inch-tall (31.1 cm) carving of a cave lion made from the tusk of a mammoth. The Lion-Man is an example of Paleolithic (Old Stone Age) art. The Venus of Hohle Fels is another example of Paleolithic sculpture that is almost as old as the Lion-Man. The tiny 2.4-inch (6 cm) female figure was discovered in another German cave in 2008.

Flash-forward to 25,000 years ago, and a Paleolithic sculptor created the Venus of Willendorf, a palm-sized limestone carving of a woman that was found in Austria in 1908. Like several other prehistoric "Venus" sculptures, the Venus of Willendorf has no face and exaggerated breasts and buttocks.

The Neolithic Period (New Stone Age) began about 11,500 years ago and lasted until about 3000 BCE. Neolithic people created many massive stone ("megalithic") monuments around the world. In Europe, two of the most famous megalithic monuments are Stonehenge in England and Carnac in France.

The oldest known sculpture, the Lion-Man of Hohlenstein-Stadel.

MEDIEVAL AND GOTHIC SCULPTORS: INSPIRED BY FAITH

The Medieval Period in Europe dates from the fall of the Roman Empire in 476 CE to the beginning of the Renaissance in the fifteenth century. Also called the Middle Ages, medieval Europe produced towering cathedrals and sculptures of saints that reflected Christian or other religious values, including those of Islam and Judaism.

A separate European artistic tradition during the Middle Ages included pagan beliefs, exemplified by the Anglo-Saxon metalwork found in the famous Sutton Hoo ship burial in England. Sutton Hoo treasures include intricate objects made from gold and silver, ranging from belt buckles to an iron helmet with a soaring dragon forming the nose and eyebrows.

Christian sculptors wanted to communicate biblical teachings to people who could not read, and they turned to stylized and illuminated (gold-covered and painted) images instead of Greek or Roman realism. In addition to cathedral doors and carved columns, artists throughout Europe carved and painted wooden crucifixes like the Gero Crucifix, displayed in Germany's Cologne Cathedral, the oldest large crucifix north of the Alps, dating from 965–70 CE.

An Anglo-Saxon helmet found in the Sutton Hoo ship burial.

BAROQUE SCULPTORS WORKED WITH PRECIOUS MATERIALS

Baroque art during the seventeenth century in Europe was, in large part, a Catholic response to the austere Reformation and Protestant movement started by Martin Luther in 1517. After a period of austerity, Catholic artists emerged in the seventeenth century with a goal of impressing and emotionally moving people through dynamic movement and elaborate ornaments. "Baroque" derives from the Spanish word for a large, irregular pearl.

Gian Lorenzo Bernini is one of the best known Baroque sculptors. His *Cathedra Petri (Chair of St. Peter)* in St. Peter's Basilica in Rome is constructed of wood, gilded bronze, gold, and stained glass to form an overwhelming impression of religious faith. Andrea Pozzo's *Saint Ignatius Chapel* in Il Gesù, Rome, was constructed and painted as a complete chapel with sculptures of saints and angels created from gold, silver, bronze, and semiprecious carved stones like lapis lazuli.

Perhaps no other structure and collection of art and sculpture represents the Baroque period in Europe better than Sun King Louis XIV's palace of Versailles, built between 1664 and 1710. Unlike the cathedrals in Rome, Versailles was devoted to the worship of France's King Louis. The chateau's many fountains celebrate Greek and Roman gods and myths, including one of the most elaborate, André Le Nôtre's *Neptune Fountain*.

The palace of Versailles was devoted to the worship of France's King Louis. The many fountains celebrate Greek and Roman gods and myths. The fountain pictured below is the Fountain of Apollo found in the gardens of the palace of Versailles.

RODIN RESPONDS TO A MODERN WORLD

The pace of life increased dramatically in nineteenth-century Europe, from the Industrial Revolution to the rise of large cities. Impressionism arose in France in the 1860s as a response to this rapid change. Auguste Rodin is the best known Impressionist sculptor. Rodin's impressionistic, emotional, and conceptual approach set him apart from more traditional sculptors. His interpretation of a man seated with his chin in his hand, *The Thinker* (1879–1889), is one of the world's best known sculptures. In 1889 Rodin completed *The Burghers of Calais*, which depicts six men of the medieval city of Calais who were asked to give up their lives, sparing the rest of the city from destruction. In Paris, Rodin's monumental sculpture of the author Balzac depicts the writer's spirit and depth of emotion.

Rodin's The Thinker.

EXPRESSIONISM: DISTORTING FORMS TO EVOKE EMOTION

Germany was one European nation rocked by change at the end of the nineteenth and beginning of the twentieth centuries. Expressionism began in Germany in the decade before World War I, as artists tried to make sense of rapidly changing morals, economic turmoil, and social structures. Expressionist sculptors were also influenced by African and Polynesian artwork brought to Europe through colonialism. One of the best-known Expressionist sculptors was Ernst Barlach, who created art before and after the First World War. His sculpture Der Geistkämpfer (*The Ghost Fighter*), created in 1928, is an antiwar image of an avenging angel with a sword standing atop a lion, echoing the famous Capitoline Wolf from Rome.

Ernst Barlach's Der Geistkämpfer depicts an avenging angel with a sword standing atop a lion.

THE 20TH CENTURY: ABSTRACT WORKS, LARGE AND SMALL

Two of the twentieth century's most celebrated sculptors could hardly have been more diverse in their approach. The Swiss sculptor Alberto Giacometti is known for his thin figures, including walking men. Among only a few animal images, Giacometti's iconic *The Cat* (1951) is a pencil-thin bronze measuring 12 inches (30.5 cm) in height and 31 inches (78.7 cm) from nose to tail.

Henry Moore, on the other hand, was a world-renowned twentieth-century British sculptor whose massive bronze and stone sculptures are displayed in public places around the world. Many of Moore's reclining figures were inspired by Mayan Chac Mool ritual stone sculptures. Few of Moore's bronze or stone sculptures are smaller than life size. The majority are much larger than life and weigh several tons.

A woman observes Giacometti's sculptures in a park in Saint-Paul-de-Vence, France.

21ST-CENTURY EUROPEAN SCULPTURE: SHOCKS AND AWES

European sculptors use traditional methods as well as twenty-first-century materials to create stunning visions from northern Europe to the Mediterranean. In 2013 the French sculptor Bruno Catalano installed 10 life-sized bronzes at the port of Marseilles that defy the imagination. Catalano's *Les Voyageurs* (*Travelers*) show ordinary people missing extraordinary parts of their bodies as they travel through the port.

The Scottish sculptor Andy Scott completed *The Kelpies* in 2014 in Falkirk, Scotland. It is the world's largest equine sculpture. Two massive horse-like kelpies, creatures from Scottish mythology, tower over the landscape; they are made from 600 tons of steel. In Prague, which is the site of many innovative sculptures, David Černý's massive head of Franz Kafka is a 39-ton moving sculpture that can be programmed for 15 different facial expressions.

Sculptor Bruno Catalano created Les Voyageurs. *One of the "travelers" he created was Van Gogh.*

CHAPTER 4 LATIN AMERICA AND THE CARIBBEAN

Between 3500 BCE and the sixteenth century, Latin American cultures created many diverse types of sculpture, from Incan monuments to Mayan Chac Mool altars, and from Moche animal sculptures to the famous Nasca lines depicting animals and gods. After Europeans arrived in the Americas, Latin American and Caribbean art changed to include Christian religious themes. From the early twentieth century onward, indigenous Latin American sculpture themes blend with Spanish and other colonial influences.

MAYAN SCULPTORS: MASTERS OF STONE AND JADE

At its greatest height, the Mayan world extended from the cities of Copan in the south to Palenque in the northwest. Today's Maya continue to speak a group of similar languages and live in Mexico, Belize, Honduras, and Guatemala. Mayan cities and monuments were built over more than 2,500 years during the Pre-Classic, Classic, and Post-Classic periods, starting in 1000 BCE up to 1521 CE.

The Mayan world was a collection of city-states in which millions of Mayans lived in independent kingdoms. Each city-state had a lord, or *ahau*, who was considered a divine ruler. Mayans created massive friezes in their temples and on steles (standing stone monuments) and calendar stones. The friezes recorded religious, military, and astronomical knowledge in Mayan glyphs, the culture's logophonetic writing system.

Mayan artists sculpted in stucco, stone, bone, shell, wood, and terra-cotta. Similar to Chinese sculptors, Mayans regarded jade as a valuable stone with religious, spiritual, and magical properties. Jade amulets, masks, and pendants were some of the most beautiful sculptures made by the Mayans. Mayan temples are some of the most extraordinary stone buildings in Mesoamerica. They included sculptures of many deities, from Chac, the

A mirror-bearer from the sixth century CE.

rain god, to Kukulkan, the feathered serpent god. Because the Mayans lived in a wet, tropical climate, however, few wooden sculptures have survived. One that did survive is the Mirror-Bearer from the sixth century CE, a wood image of a court jester who bore a polished stone mirror to reflect the face of the *ahau* of his city.

Many of the most intricate Mayan stone carvings are deep reliefs that adorned lintels on temples and ceremonial buildings. Reliefs from the lintels of Yaxchilan in Chiapas, Mexico, show the Mayan blood ritual, in which noble men and women pulled thorned cords through their tongues to sacrifice blood for spiritual purposes.

This relief from the lintels of Yaxchilan depicts the vision of bloodletting. It is believed to come from the Mayan Empire, 700 CE.

THE INCA: ART FROM STONE, GOLD, AND SILVER

Visitors to Peru today marvel at the stone monuments of Incan culture. The Inca established an empire in the Andes in South America between 1300 and 1532 CE, when the Spanish conquistador Pizarro took the Inca ruler Atahualpa hostage. The Inca kingdom was both rocky and mountainous, and, at its greatest extent, it stretched from Quito in modern-day Ecuador to Santiago, at the tip of Chile.

The Inca created many artworks from gold and silver. Small human figures made from precious metals were dressed in clothing and buried at the site of human sacrifices on the highest mountain peaks. Animal figures may have had spiritual meaning or even been decorative items or toys. The Inca put wheels on ceramic children's toys, but they didn't use the wheel for work. The reason was practical: The narrow Inca roads were meant for official government business. The Inca also used alpacas and llamas for transport, but the maximum weight they can carry or pull is about 100 pounds (45 kg). Human and alpaca foot power was superior to wheels and carts on steep mountain pathways.

Machu Pichu.

The Inca constructed buildings from massive blocks of stone fitted together with a stonemason's skill and designed to resist earthquakes. They required no mortar, an approach that astonishes Andean visitors today for its ingenuity and beauty. From the high mountain royal retreat of Machu Picchu to the fortress of Sacsayhuamán outside Cusco, Inca stone carvings were often small, in contrast to their monumental buildings. Small jade and limestone carvings depict male and female ancestors with anatomically correct body parts. The Intihuatana stone at Machu Picchu looks like a contemporary abstract stone sculpture, but it represented far more than that to the Inca. Dedicated to the Inca's creator god Viracocha, the stone provided astronomical observations and had spiritual importance. The Inca also carved intricate stone vessels for ceremonial purposes, often decorated with the three animals most closely associated with their culture and empire: the condor, the snake, and the puma.

The Incan people used stones as a precise indicator of time and date. This clock is located at the Central Plaza in Machu Pichu.

MESOAMERICAN SCULPTURE: DIVERSE CULTURES AND BELIEFS

Native people in Mexico began to raise an early form of corn called *teosinte* about 7,000 years ago, which led quickly to the formation of towns, and eventually cultures and city-states. The earliest major civilization in Mesoamerica was that of the Olmecs, who lived in today's Mexican states of Veracruz and Tabasco.

The Olmecs had a sophisticated civilization with highly skilled artisans. Best known for their massive helmeted heads, some up to 11 feet (3.3 m) in height and weighing as much as 55 tons (49,895.2 kg). Art historians believe that the Olmec heads represented rulers wearing helmets meant for the Mesoamerican ballgame, a sport that was played throughout the region for thousands of years. The Olmecs also carved jade masks and amulets. They were experienced in creating whiteware ceramics of lifelike figurines with a "baby face." The figures

The Olmec heads can be found throughout Mexico.

look like infants but may represent an adult or a god—their meaning has been lost to time.

Other Mesoamerican cultures include the Tlatilco, who lived in the Valley of Mexico between 1500 and 800 BCE, long before the Aztecs (also called Mexica). Tlatilco people made many ceramic figurines that show both a sense of humor and creativity. Many Tlatilco figurines are unique, but none are as unusual as a double-faced female figurine with three eyes, two noses, and two mouths, created 2,500 years ago.

The Aztecs came much later than the Tlatilco or Olmecs. Their empire was centered in Tenochtitlan, founded in 1325 CE at the site of present-day Mexico City. Aztec architecture was monumental, featuring palaces for nobles and temples devoted to deities. Aztec sculpture continues to be unearthed in Mexico City, and sites like the Plaza Mayor and Temple Mayor are incorporated into Mexico City's ongoing life. Aztec stoneworkers were highly skilled, creating masterworks like a 10-foot-tall (3 m) Coatlicue, a female deity with a skirt made of snakes and a skull belt buckle.

The Aztec's Coatlicue stands 10 feet tall with a skirt made of snakes and a skull belt buckle.

Teotihuacan: The Oldest City in the Americas

The monumental pyramids of Teotihuacan, located about 25 miles (40 km) northeast of Mexico City, were not built by the Aztecs. They were built more than 1,000 years before the Aztecs arrived. Some cultural influences represented in the city's ruins include the Toltecs, Totonacs, Mixtecs, Zapotecs, and Maya. The wide main street of Teotihuacan is called the Street of the Dead, and its largest pyramid was the tallest structure in North or South America until modern construction began.

Teotihuacan sculptures of Quetzalcoatl (the Feathered Serpent) and skulls and rulers have themes in common with many Mesoamerican cultures. Teotihuacan's ruins cover 8 square miles (12.8 sq km). The scale of its buildings and roads, all built by hand, were so awesome that when their abandoned ruins were discovered by the Aztecs in the fourteenth century, the Aztecs named them "City of the Gods," or *Teotihuacan* in Nahuatl, the Aztec language.

Detail from the Temple of Quetzalcoatl at Teotihuacan outside Mexico City.

TIWANAKU'S MYSTERIOUS STONE MONOLITHS

Tiwanaku is an ancient city in the Bolivian Andes that is 13,000 feet (4,000 m) above sea level near Lake Titicaca, making it one of the highest-elevation cities ever built. It was built by the Tiwanaku people—a mysterious pre-Inca civilization—between 500 and 1000 CE. The Tiwanaku people were accomplished stone masons and builders, erecting numerous temples and ceremonial pyramids. Stones found on an unfinished platform called *Pumapunku* are carved with elaborate and precise geometric patterns. Sunken temples feature walls decorated with Expressionistic carved faces that represent deities and demons.

The largest sculptures at Tiwanaku are monoliths standing 19–23 feet (6–7 m) tall that represent guardian deities. Each monolith is carved out of volcanic rock and holds a goblet in its left hand. Researchers think the goblet might have held *chicha*, a fermented drink still enjoyed in the area today. A smaller form of sculpture at Tiwanaku is the *chachapuma*, a human–puma (mountain lion) spirit that holds an axe in one hand and a severed human head in the other.

The monoliths at Tiwanaku are carved out of volcanic rock.

THE MADONNA AND VIRGIN OF GUADALUPE'S ENDURING LEGACY

Art, culture, and many other aspects of life for the people of Latin America changed after the Spanish conquered Mesoamerica and South America. Today's Mexico was called "New Spain," and all of South America except present-day Brazil was named the Viceroyalty of Peru. Franciscan Catholic missionaries landed in 1523, followed by Dominicans, Augustinians, and Jesuits.

Mission schools in Mexico and Peru taught indigenous people European art traditions as well as Christian religion. One such convert was Juan Diego, an Aztec who witnessed two visions of the Virgin Mary in December 1531. Mary asked Juan to build a church near Mexico City. When Juan told the Spanish bishop about the Virgin Mary's request, the bishop requested more proof. After the second vision, Juan returned to the bishop and opened his cloak to reveal dozens of roses and Mary's image imprinted on the fabric. The church was built, and thousands of images of Our Lady of Guadalupe, Mexico's patron saint, have since been carved and painted throughout Mexico and Latin America.

Statues of Our Lady of Guadalupe are commonly seen throughout Mexico, especially near or inside churches.

BRASÍLIA: A CAPITAL PLANNED FROM START TO FINISH

Brasília is the newest major world capital city, founded in 1960 to serve as Brazil's new capital. The city is a planned community

Justice stands in front of Brazil's Supreme Federal Court building.

developed by Lúcio Costa and Oscar Niemeyer. UNESCO named Brasília a City of Design in 2017 because of its unique construction and urban environment.

Many of Brasília's planned buildings and public squares feature public sculpture installations, including Praça dos Tres Poderes (Square of the Three Powers). Bruno Giorgi's large abstract stone sculpture *Meteor* rests in a reflecting pool near the Foreign Ministry in the Praça. In the center of the Praça stands Giorgi's *Os Candangos*, a monumental bronze commemorating the workers who built the city. A white granite female *Justice* by Alfredo Ceschiatti stands in front of Brazil's Supreme Federal Court building.

MEXICO'S SOCIAL AWAKENING

Social Realism was a world art movement that occurred in the early to mid-twentieth century, and in Mexico, artists were inspired to create art celebrating the people and their struggles during, and for decades after, the 1910–1920 Mexican Revolution. Many of the Mexican Social Realists artists were best known as mural painters, but some expanded their murals into 3-D painted reliefs. One of the most famous examples is David Alfaro Siqueiros's mural celebrating the connection between the Mexican people and the national university in Mexico City, a relief mosaic built between 1952 and 1956.

David Alfaro Siqueiros's mural celebrating the connection between the Mexican people and the national university.

FERNANDO BOTERO: LARGER-THAN-LIFE SCULPTURES

A Fernando Botero statue on display.

Looking carefully, viewers can see echoes of Olmec "baby face" whiteware ceramics and other pre-Columbian Latin American civilizations in the larger-than-life images of Colombian artist Fernando Botero. Born in 1932 in Medellin, Colombia, Botero is one of the world's best known painters and sculptors. His sculptures are frequently of women, including mothers and children and women riding horses. Botero's style is referred to as "volumetric stylization," exaggerating the size and weight of humans and animals. Some believe Botero is making a commentary on a greedy society, while others see humor and beauty in his style.

UNDERWATER SCULPTURES

A worldwide tourist destination for its clear blue waters, underwater reefs, and snorkeling, the Caribbean entered the twenty-first century pioneering a new way to create and enjoy sculpture: the underwater sculpture garden. The first Caribbean underwater sculpture was erected in 2000 at the Sunset House Resort in Grand Cayman: a 9-foot-tall (2.7 m) bronze statue of Amphitrite, the legendary queen of the sea. Mexico's Isla Mujeres near Cancun hosts the Museo Subacuático de Arte, with over 500 life-sized sculptures in a natural coral reef. The largest underwater sculpture is a 60-ton Bahamian girl called *Ocean Atlas*, located off New Providence Island in the Bahamas.

A diver swims next to Ocean Atlas off the coast of New Providence Island in the Bahamas.

CHAPTER 5 MIDDLE EAST

The Middle East covers parts of three continents: western Asia, North Africa, and southeastern Europe. Civilization and sculpture in the region include some of the world's oldest cities and iconic sculptural traditions, from Egyptian monuments to ancient Persian kingdoms, and the 12,000-year-old temples discovered at the archaeological site of Göbekli Tepe in Turkey.

THE ANCIENT MIDDLE EAST: BIRTHPLACE OF STONE MONUMENTS AND SCULPTURE

First excavated in 1995, the ancient Turkish temple site called Göbekli Tepe has singlehandedly rewritten many art and archaeology textbooks. Circular temple enclosures surround more than 200 T-shaped carved stone pillars. The pillars are up to 18 feet (5.5 m) tall and weigh as much as 16 tons (14,515 kg). Some of the pillars depict people with hands, belts, buckles, and loincloths. Others feature detailed bas-reliefs of animals, including vultures, scorpions, and cattle. Göbekli Tepe ("Potbelly Hill") is dated to 10,000 BCE, or more than 12,000 years ago, even before agriculture is believed to have been invented.

Also in Turkey, the ancient city of Çatalhöyük shows how important sculpture and art was to the daily lives of the residents of the 9,000-year-old city. Nearly every home that has been excavated has plaster bas-reliefs, and several sculpted stone religious figures, including female goddesses, have been uncovered.

Göbekli Tepe is a circular temple with more than 200 T-shaped carved stone pillars.

Steles are carved stones that are taller than they are wide. They are commonly used as grave markers or memorials. The deep sands of the Arabian Desert hid a few steles depicting simple male figures that have recently been uncovered and date from the fourth millennium BCE in Saudi Arabia.

The earliest Middle Eastern military empire was Akkad, located between the Tigris and Euphrates Rivers in ancient Mesopotamia. The Akkadian ruler Sargon founded the kingdom in 2300 BCE, and a bronze head of an Akkadian ruler has created the image of a stern, bearded Sargon we know today. The Akkadians created memorial steles of their victories. One of the best known of these is the Victory Stele of Naram-Sin, which combines writing and bas-relief battle scenes.

The Sumerians, who followed the Akkadians in ruling the region, are the people who built the city of Ur and its famous ziggurat, a massive terraced temple. The Sumerians invented cuneiform writing around 3500 BCE. A 3-foot-tall (93 cm) statue of the Sumerian prince Gudea, Architect with Plan, illustrates the value Sumerians placed on writing and architecture. It is made of a rare, hard-to-carve stone called "diorite."

The 3-foot-tall statue of prince Gudea is on display at the Louvre.

THE SCULPTURE OF ANCIENT EGYPT

For more than 4,000 years, no structure on earth was taller than Egypt's Great Pyramid in Giza. The civilization of the ancient Egyptians lasted for over 3,000 years, centered on the Nile River. Egyptian art, especially sculpture, remained consistent throughout the civilization's long history. Egypt's combination of desert weather, artistry in durable stone, and cultural longevity combined to create one of the world's most familiar and influential art and cultural traditions.

One of the oldest Egyptian sculptures is the 5,200-year-old Narmer Palette, which shows the first ruler of Upper and Lower Egypt. Carved from siltstone, the palette has an image of Narmer on both sides, along with some of the earliest examples of hieroglyphic writing. The Egyptian Old Kingdom dates to about 400 years after Narmer and is the period when the Great Pyramids of Giza were built, as well as the Great Sphinx. The Great Sphinx, with the body of a lion and the head of an Egyptian pharaoh, is 240 feet (73 m) long and 66.3 feet (20.2 m) tall.

In Egypt's long history, a few women ruled by themselves as pharaoh, but one of the most famous and powerful was Queen Hatshepsut, who became pharaoh in 1478 BCE during Egypt's New Kingdom Period. Hatshepsut's memorial temple is one of the most beautiful and graceful Egyptian stone structures. Within the

The Narmer Palette is carved from siltstone. There is a front and back, which shows the first ruler of Upper and Lower Egypt.

The memorial temple for Queen Hatshepsut was built between the cliffs on the west bank of the Nile River.

temple are many examples of New Kingdom sculpting skill, including a kneeling statue of Hatshepsut made from polished pink granite. Although she was a queen, Hatshepsut's statue wears the false beard of a male pharaoh.

The New Kingdom was also the time of Tutankhamun, a teenage pharaoh whose name might have been forgotten by history if his tomb full of stunning treasures had not been discovered in Egypt's Valley of the Kings in 1922. "King Tut" was the son of the rebel pharaoh Akhenaten, who is remembered for launching a short-lived religion of sun worship and building Amarna, a new royal city in the desert. Akhenaten's wife, Nefertiti (stepmother of Tutankhamun), is the subject of one of the most famous sculptures and depictions of female beauty in history: the bust of Nefertiti created by the sculptor Thutmose in 1345 BCE.

Egyptian Painters and Sculptors Were Also Scribes

A detailed, painted limestone sculpture of an Egyptian scribe created during Egypt's Old Kingdom in about 2600 BCE provides a glimpse of the profession of scribe in ancient Egypt. Scribes performed many governmental, financial, and religious duties because they knew how to write in Egypt's hieroglyphic script. If we examine any ancient Egyptian paintings, reliefs, or carvings, they are never without hieroglyphic inscriptions.

The Egyptians believed that an image without words was incomplete, just as words without an image were not meaningful or alive. Much of Egyptian life was oriented toward the afterlife, as shown by the complex rituals prescribed in the Egyptian *Book of the Dead*. Sculptors and painters needed to have artistic skill and training, as well as to know how to write inscriptions to make their creations complete in the world of the living—as well as the world of the dead.

PERSIAN SCULPTURE HAS A 6,000-YEAR HISTORY

The ancient city of Susa, or Shushan, in Iran was settled as early as 4200 BCE and is the site of monumental stone and bronze sculptures and decorative friezes made from bright glazed bricks. Sculptures from over 3,500 years of history have been recovered from archaeological expeditions to Susa, which has been named a UNESCO World Heritage site. Although Susa was and is an Iranian or Persian city, at times in its history it was under Akkadian, Babylonian, and Greek (Macedonian) rule.

Many terra-cotta figurines have been found in Susa that represent figures of goddesses and gods used by individual worshippers. Many depict the goddess Inanna or other female deities, including some with exaggerated hips and thighs, indicating fertility. Two periods of the powerful Persian Empire created sculpture and art, about 500 years apart. The first Persian Empire was founded by Cyrus

Susa, Iran is home to the traditional burial place of the biblical prophet Daniel.

Persepolis is a UNESCO World Heritage site.

the Great. Also called the Achaemenid Empire, it lasted from 550 to 330 BCE and was the largest in the world during its time. The successor to Cyrus, Darius the Great, built Persepolis, the great imperial Persian capital. In the time of Darius, Persia was able to create solid gold sculptures of royal winged lions and an infinite variety of gold decorative items and jewelry. One famous group of Persian gold reliefs, figurines, and jewelry is the 180-piece Oxus Treasure.

The second Persian Empire was the Sassanid Empire, which lasted from 200 to 650 CE. The Sassanid capital was Ctesiphon in present-day Iraq. Along with many half and full arches, Ctesephon's buildings included blind arches, an echo of Roman architecture. Reliefs at Persepolis show uniquely Persian designs, such as repeating floral images, equestrian images of conquerors on horseback, and exotic scenes of the far-flung Persian Empire, including elephants from India. The horse is an ever-present theme in Persian sculpture, as is the winged lion, a symbol of imperial power and might.

CARTHAGE'S SCULPTURAL HERITAGE

The ancient city of Carthage was located on the coast of North Africa in present-day Tunisia. Carthage was settled by Phoenician traders from the Lebanese coastal city of Tyre in the ninth century BCE. The Phoenicians were worldwide traders and seafarers, and they brought many goods, materials, and cultural influences home to their seaside port city.

By the middle of the second century BCE, the Roman Republic had become more powerful, and it wanted to possess Carthage's territory around the Mediterranean. Carthage fought a series of three wars with the Romans, ending in the city's destruction in 146 BCE.

Carthage's religion, culture, and artworks were devastated by the Romans. But the artifacts that remain show a lively and imaginative culture. Carthaginian masks decorated homes and gravesites, expressing fear and humor. Although Carthage borrowed many techniques of Greek art, they never created nude statues of males or females. Even goddess figurines were clothed, as were images of Carthage's god, Ba'al. The Carthaginians made unique painted clay and glass paste jewelry that featured masks of humans and animals for good luck and to ward off evil.

This mosaic found in Carthage depicts the masks used by actors in tragedies and comedies.

PETRA: A CITY IN STONE

The Nabateans were a wealthy, thriving people who lived in cities between the Sinai Desert and Arabia between about 400 BCE and the second century CE. The Nabateans' best known city, Petra, lay hidden from most people in the outside world for centuries after the Roman Emperor Trajan annexed the Nabatean Kingdom in 106 CE. Accessed only through a narrow, curving canyon called the Siq, Petra's buildings are all carved directly from the desert canyon rock.

Today, Petra is a World Heritage site in Jordan, and travelers come from all over the world to see its amazing buildings. Carved in Greek-inspired arches and columns, some of Petra's structures are tombs, while others are temples. At its height, more than 20,000 people may have lived in Petra, which was a luxurious city with abundant water. The Nabateans brought life-giving water from distant cliffs and hills using an ingenious gravity-fed water system.

A monastery is built into the side of a cliff in Petra.

LIONS: A SYMBOL OF POWER

Lions no longer live in the Middle East, but until the 1960s, Barbary lions survived in North Africa and Egypt. Asiatic lions once roamed between the Middle East and India, but only a few of them survive today in an Indian game preserve. The lion has been a symbol of power, kingship, and strength in the Middle East for millennia, attested to by the 10,000-year-old sculptures found on the T-shaped stone pillars at Göbekli Tepe in Turkey.

A seventh century BCE bas-relief sculpture from the royal Assyrian palace of Nineveh depicts King Ashurbanipal killing captured lions to show his power and privilege. Maahes was the Egyptian lion god of war, depicted in many bas-reliefs and freestanding sculptures. The Great Sphinx at Giza combines the head of a pharaoh and the body of a lion. Persian kings used lions as their symbols, and hundreds of lion images have been found in Persian bas-reliefs and on bronze, stone, and precious metal sculptures.

The Assyrian chariot lion hunt.

CLEOPATRA'S UNDERWATER PALACE

One of history's greatest generals, Macedonian Alexander the Great, conquered Egypt in 332 BCE. When one of Alexander's generals became the Egyptian Emperor Ptolemy, Egypt's last pharaonic dynasty began, lasting until 30 BCE at the death of Ptolemy's descendant, Cleopatra. Cleopatra's capital city was Alexandria, which was founded by Alexander in 331 BCE.

Alexandria's Abu Qir Bay hid relics of Cleopatra's palace underwater for over 1,400 years. Along with blocks of the city's ancient Pharos lighthouse, considered one of the Wonders of the Ancient World, more than 2,500

The death of Cleopatra marked the end of Egypt's last pharaonic dynasty.

sculptures and columns from Cleopatra's reign are underwater. Egypt plans an underwater museum to showcase the relics, but currently only snorkelers and glass-bottomed boats can glimpse the treasures.

KING ANTIOCHUS'S PALACE MONUMENTS STILL IMPRESS

In the first century BCE, King Antiochus, son of King Mithridates, was one of the ancient world's wealthiest monarchs. His tomb on top of Mount Nemrut in Turkey is in ruins, but the monumental stone heads of the king and mythical figures are still impressive, even scattered on the ground. When the statues were erected, they stood 26–29 feet (8–9 m) high. Massive

The monumental stone heads of King Antiochus and mythical figures.

stone lions and eagles guarded the tomb. Along with King Antiochus, statues of several of his ancestors guarded the site, but today the heads rest on the ground away from the pedestals where their bodies once stood.

THE ANCIENT PLASTER ARTISTS OF AYN GHAZAL

About 9,000 years ago, Neolithic artists in Jordan created unusual and mysterious statues made from reeds and plaster. Jordanian highway developers uncovered the prehistoric site while building a highway through Ayn Ghazal in the 1970s. Fifteen standing statues and 15 sculptured busts were discovered. Some of the statues are two-headed (bicephalous), featuring two realistically sculpted heads and necks on a single wide-shouldered body. Other bodies have realistic heads but wide hips and legs and no arms. The sculptures used an armature (framework), which helped them to stand on their own, but they were meant to be viewed only from the front, because their back sides are blank and incomplete.

One of the 15 plaster busts of Ayn Ghazal.

SCULPTORS OF THE ARAB SPRING

In the seventh century, Muslims conquered Persia, and the Islamic influence in the Middle East spread. Because the Qu'ran forbids the depiction of realistic images, particularly paintings and sculptures of people, this affected the visual arts. In 2010 a series of demonstrations and protests occurred throughout the Arab world, known as the Arab Spring. Since that time, sculptors in the Arab world have become more comfortable in creating sculpture that obeys the Qu'ran yet presents artistic creativity. Monir Shahroudy Farmanfarmaian is a sculptor in Dubai who creates intricate geometric shapes. The Lebanese sculptor Saloua Raouda Choucair creates sculptures from interlocking geometric forms.

A sculpture by Lebanese artist Saloua Raouda Choucair.

CHAPTER 6 NORTH AMERICA

North America includes Canada, the United States, and Mexico, but the art traditions of Mexico are more closely aligned with Latin America. Native people in Canada, Alaska, and the continental United States have created sculpture for spiritual and cultural purposes for thousands of years. American sculpture was in the shadow of European sculpture during Revolutionary War days, but by the nineteenth century it had begun to achieve its own distinctive themes, including a celebration of the animals and images of the American West.

NATIVE AMERICAN SCULPTURAL TRADITIONS: CELEBRATING NATURE AND SPIRITUALITY

Native Americans may have lived in North America as long as 23,000 years ago. This is significantly farther in the past than the Clovis culture, long reported to be the first group of Native Americans to arrive in North America by walking across a land bridge from Siberia 13,000 years ago. Native Americans say they have always lived in North America.

Among the earliest types of Native American sculptures were fetishes, which are small carvings of animals that may be used in religious ceremonies or to provide good luck, health, or protection. Today, the best known fetishes are those made by the Zuni, which call them *Ahlashiwe*. Fetishes usually have a carved and inlaid or painted heart line, which represents the life spirit of the animal.

Small fetishes could be held in the palm of the hand, but Native Americans also sculpted the land itself in natural forms. The Great Serpent Mound in Ohio is a 437-yard-long (400 m) snake embedded in a grass-covered hill, created by the Fort Ancient culture in the tenth century. The Mississippian culture, which

The Great Serpent Mound in Ohio.

lasted from 800 to 1600 CE, built the large city of Cahokia near present-day St. Louis, Missouri. In addition to earth pyramids and mounds, Mississippians created elaborate copper plates depicting rulers and religious figures and stone carvings of men and women at work. Clay effigy pipes such as the Lucifer from Spiro express mysterious emotions that are difficult to understand over 1,000 years after they were created.

Many people have seen Hopi *kachina* dolls, which are not toys but were used to teach children about *kachinas*, also called *katsinas*. *Kachinas* are carved from cottonwood root and painted to represent more than 500 different spirits that communicate with humans and provide natural blessings.

Another ancient tradition that continued into the eighteenth and nineteenth centuries is the carving of petroglyphs, or rock art. Native Americans throughout the Southwest carved images of animals and abstract symbols into desert or canyon rocks, either in impressive open galleries or in hidden canyons.

A traditional Hopi kachina doll.

AMERICAN SCULPTURE IN THE 19TH CENTURY

The founders of the United States turned to ancient Rome for inspiration for the new nation, and for much of the architecture and sculpture in the nation's new capital, Washington, DC. George Washington engaged the French expatriate Pierre L'Enfant to design the new nation's capital, centered on the National Mall, designed to be a public walk. Washington is designed on the principle that every citizen is equally important.

Most of the buildings in Washington, from the Capitol to the Washington Monument, are inspired by buildings of the ancient world. The revival architecture is called Neoclassicism, and the theme was also reflected in most nineteenth-century American sculpture. Hiram Powers became one of the most famous nineteenth-century American sculptors. Working in marble, his depiction of *The Greek Slave* inspired a poem by Elizabeth Barrett Browning. *The Greek Slave* looks like Classical Greek and Roman nude statues, except for the slave's intricately

America's Monuments: Commemorating Ideals and Fallen Leaders

Ancient Egyptians erected funerary monuments to their leaders, from the Great Pyramid of Giza to the mortuary temple of Queen Hatshepsut. Romans built triumphal arches and temples to gods, including emperors like Augustus. The United States has built monuments, but the emphasis is different from that of many cultures of the past. America's best known monuments aren't religious, and they don't tend to celebrate military triumphs.

The Lincoln Memorial commemorates the memory of one of America's greatest presidents, assassinated before he could oversee the peace after America's Civil War. The statue of Abraham Lincoln in the memorial is 19 feet (5.8 m) tall. Designed by the sculptor Daniel Chester French, the statue was assembled from 28 pieces carved from white marble. Dedicated in 1886, the *Statue of Liberty* represents the concept of liberty and freedom, towering over New York Harbor. Mount Rushmore in South Dakota, designed by Gutzon Borglum, is carved out of the Black Hills themselves. Although the monument draws hundreds of thousands of visitors a year, it is unfinished.

carved wrist irons and chains. John Quincy Adams Ward sculpted many American figures, from a larger-than-life statue of George Washington in New York City to *The Freedman*, an image of an African American who has freed himself from slavery, created and exhibited in the middle of the U.S. Civil War in 1863.

One of the world's most famous and largest statues, the *Statue of Liberty*, also echoes Neoclassical themes. The statue, designed by the French sculptor Frédéric Auguste Bartholdi, represents Libertas, the Roman goddess of liberty, and was dedicated in 1886. The 305-foot (93 m) statue is made of copper. Its interior and frame were built by Gustave Eiffel, who was also the builder of Paris's Eiffel Tower.

During the second half of the nineteenth century, American sculptors began to sculpt themes unknown in Europe, including the American bison and Native Americans. Monumental sculpture, from the Lincoln Memorial to Mount Rushmore, became an American art form. Whereas in Asia, monumental sculptures were created of Buddha, and in the Middle East, of pharaohs and emperors, U.S. monumental sculpture featured presidents and idealized figures representing liberty and justice.

The Statue of Liberty *is still an iconic image as people enter the New York Harbor.*

THE AMERICAN FRONTIER AND THE MYTH OF THE WILD WEST

The settling of America's frontier began after the Revolutionary War in the 1780s and continued until the early days of the twentieth century. Known as the "Old West" or "Wild West," the experiences of cowboys, settlers, Native Americans, and others in the lands west of the Mississippi River inspired the creation of Western-themed American art, including sculpture. Books and Hollywood films told iconic, if unrealistic, stories about cowboys, Indians, and frontier life. America's Western sculptors had a romantic quality, but they also worked from photographs and in-person observations of living cowboys, bucking broncos, and Native Americans.

Charles Marion Russell was one of the best known artists chronicling the Wild West. Russell left school at age 16 and went to Montana to work on a sheep ranch, earning the nickname "Kid" Russell. Most of Russell's sculptures were cast in bronze and meant to be displayed in family homes, not art museums. Russell lived most of his life in Great Falls, Montana, where he became a celebrated figure. His sculptures include animals such as wolves, bison, and bighorn sheep; Native

Charles Marion Russell's Meat for Wild Men *depicts a buffalo hunt.*

Americans; and cowboys in action, from bucking broncos to roping steers. He also created intricate scenes of stagecoaches and mule trains.

Another noted sculptor of the American West was Frederic Remington. Remington and Russell were almost the same age: Both were born during the Civil War. Whereas Russell left school as a teenager and went to work on a sheep ranch, Remington was born in New York and attended Yale University. Trips to the West inspired Remington to paint and create sculpture commemorating open spaces, cowboys, cattle, and Native Americans. One of Remington's sculptures, *The Broncho*

Frederic Remington's The Broncho Buster.

Buster (1895), shows a cowboy taming a wild, rearing horse. President Teddy Roosevelt's Rough Rider cavalry regiment gifted him with the sculpture, contributing to Remington's fame and greatly pleasing their famous leader.

Western-themed sculptures have a sense of action and movement that wasn't present in Neoclassical busts inspired by ancient Roman art. Some historians have written that America is the only nation to live and create its own mythology at the same time, and Western sculptors played a large role in this process.

INUIT SCULPTURE AND THE NORTHERN ECONOMY

The Inuit people in Canada and Alaska live in arctic and subarctic climates. Their traditional cold-weather clothing includes the parka, which is now worn worldwide. The Inuit fish and hunt caribou, seal, whale, and smaller animals and birds. Their lifestyles inspire their sculpture, which has changed over the years. Prehistoric Inuit sculpture was made of bone, ivory, or stone, and it was small, because early Inuit had no permanent homes, so anything they created had to be carried with them.

During the period of contact with southern whalers and traders, Inuit people began to carve bone or stone artwork for trading with the outside world. Although these carvings included scenes of Inuit life and animals familiar to them, the Inuit also created items like dice and chess pieces. In 1949 an Inuit sculptor named James Houston exhibited carvings in Montreal, resulting in the Canadian government sponsoring Inuit art cooperatives to bring economic development to northern communities. Inuit sculpture became so popular that traditional ivory couldn't meet the demand, so soapstone became the new basic material used by most artists. Inuit soapstone carvings are some of the most sought-after decorative sculptures today.

An Inuit carving on display in Quebec, Canada.

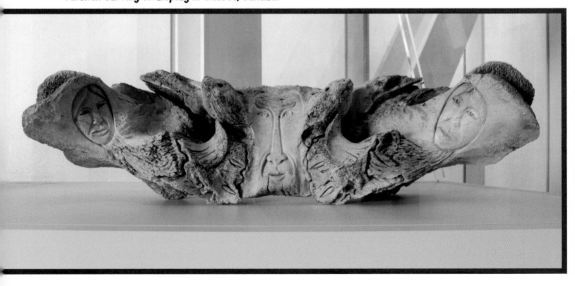

AUGUSTUS SAINT-GAUDENS, SCULPTOR OF THE BEAUX-ARTS AMERICAN RENAISSANCE

Augustus Saint-Gaudens was born in Dublin, Ireland, in 1848, but he was brought to the United States as an infant and raised in New York City. His sculptures during the second half of the nineteenth century embody the spirit of America's renaissance of art and culture that regarded the United States as the heir to Rome, Greece, and the Italian Renaissance. Saint-Gaudens created dozens of memorials, primarily of the Civil War era. The best known of these is the *Robert Gould Shaw Memorial*, located on Boston Common. The memorial is a bronze relief flanked by Classical marble columns. It commemorates the Union army regiment led by Robert Gould Shaw, which consisted of all African American free soldiers.

Saint-Gaudens also sculpted *Diana*, an interpretation of the Greek goddess of the hunt, which was originally displayed on top of Madison Square Garden in New York City. A restored, gilded version of *Diana* is displayed in the Philadelphia Museum of Art, and dozens of other copies are in museums and estates around the United States. Saint-Gaudens also designed one of the most beautiful special-issue U.S. gold coins, the 1907 high-relief $20 gold double eagle.

In the center of Grand Army Plaza in New York City stands Saint-Gaudens's William Tecumseh Sherman Monument.

ALEXANDER CALDER: INVENTOR OF THE MOBILE

Alexander Calder was born in 1898, but his art is some of the most iconic of the mid-twentieth century. Although his mother was a painter and father a sculptor, Calder did not plan to be an artist, but an engineer. As a young man, Calder worked on a ship sailing from New York to San Francisco, where he woke to see a sunrise on one side of the ship and a full moon on the other. He was so impressed by the sight that he resolved to become an artist.

From an early age, Calder created objects out of metal and wire that represented abstract shapes, not recognizable figurative art. He created his first kinetic (moving) sculpture, made of moving, connected shapes, in 1931. When the avant-garde artist Marcel Duchamp saw it, he called it a "mobile," coining a word to describe a completely new form of sculpture. Nonmoving sculptures by Calder, which he also created, were thereafter called "stable." Calder created mobiles of all sizes, from small and personal to monumental. He was one of the most famous and renowned artists in the world by the 1960s. His sculpture *Man*, created for the 1967 Montreal Expo, is one of his largest works at 65 feet (19.8 m) tall.

Alexander Calder's Man.

MAMAN, THE GIANT SPIDER

Made of stainless steel, marble, and bronze, a 30-foot-tall (10 m) spider has greeted visitors to Canada's National Gallery in Ottawa since 1999. Few who see *Maman*, created by the French-American sculptor Louise Bourgeois, fail to have an emotional response. *Ma-*

Ottawa's landmark, Maman.

man means "mother" in French, and the sculpture has some inspiration from Bourgeois's mother, who was a weaver. The giant spider has a steel net abdomen, which is filled with 26 marble eggs. Although *Maman* is now a landmark in Ottawa, some Canadians questioned the National Gallery's $3.2 million purchase of the massive sculpture. *Maman* is also not unique: The original iron version is at London's Tate Gallery, along with six other replicas at other world museums. Louise Bourgeois was one of the most noted abstract artists of the twentieth century, along with Mark Rothko and Jackson Pollock, and one of the first female internationally acclaimed large-scale sculptors.

THE HYPERREALISM OF DUANE HANSON

Although the sculptor never meant for his artwork to deceive visitors to art museums, Minnesota native Duane Hanson's hyperrealistic sculptures of everyday people are so detailed that thousands of museumgoers have walked past or sat beside them, not realizing they were museum exhibits instead of living people. Hanson began his technique of emphasizing extreme Realism in the 1960s by making casts of real people using fiberglass and vinyl. He not only painted and refined the underlying sculptures, he also dressed them in clothing from secondhand stores. Dozens of Hanson sculptures in museums around the world can be seen on exhibit sitting on benches, standing in corners, or positioned as if they are viewing other works of art.

Duane Hanson's Lonesome Cowboy.

FACTS ABOUT TOTEM POLES

Totem poles in Vancouver, Canada.

In the Pacific Northwest, Canada, and Alaska, few sculptures are more familiar than the totem pole, examples of which are created by nearly every tribe in the region. Totem poles are carved from the trunks of trees. Their meanings vary depending on the creator's interest and the pole's purpose. They can be decorative, serve as a part of a house, or be a memorial marker for an individual or family. Characters like the Thunderbird, Raven, and Beaver are portrayed consistently enough to be recognized, no matter which artist carved the poles.

Robert Smithson's Spiral Jetty.

ROBERT SMITHSON: SCULPTURE OUT OF THE LAND AND SEA

The twentieth-century American artist and author Robert Smithson had a unique vision for his art. Although he did not limit himself to large works of art created from earth and water, he is best known for earthworks like the *Spiral Jetty*, which he created at Utah's Great Salt Lake in 1970. Smithson was inspired to create works of art from earth and water, coining the term "land art" after seeing the Great Serpent Mound in Ohio. He used many large and small tools, including dump trucks, to create his assemblages of natural materials. He also brought materials like soil and sand indoors to combine into "nonsites," which were interior reflections of exterior locations. Nonsites and other interior assemblages often included mirrors, many of which the artist cracked and covered with dust, sand, and debris.

CHAPTER 7 OCEANIA

Oceania is the region of the earth that has the largest amount of water compared to land mass. The largest land mass in Oceania is Australia. Polynesia, Micronesia, and Melanesia are also part of Oceania. Traditions of sculpture in Oceania are diverse and include Polynesian tiki, indigenous Australian rock carvings, the massive ancestor *moai* of Easter Island, and Indonesian depictions of the Buddha.

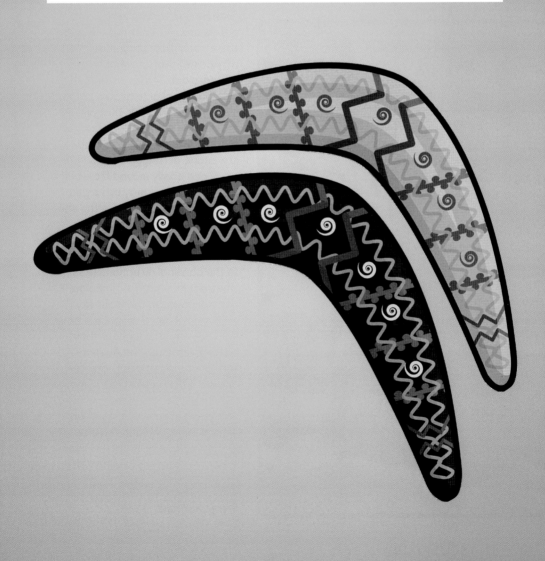

AUSTRALIA'S ABORIGINAL ROCK ART

Indigenous people have lived in Australia for at least 60,000 years, and some research indicates they may have lived on the island continent for as long as 100,000 years. Rock art created by Australian aboriginal people and Torres Strait Islanders (related, but distinctly different people) dates back at least 40,000 years. Murujuga or Burrup rock art, located on islands off the Pilbara coast in Western Australia, is some of the oldest, most famous early Australian carving. Australian rock carvers created an astonishing 1 million petroglyphs on standing stones at Murujuga. The petroglyphs appear on nearly every exposed rock in the

archipelago, including realistic depictions of sea turtles and the extinct Tasmanian tiger (thylacine) that are thousands of years old.

Aboriginal artists also created stone arrangements that are associated with spiritual traditions, ceremonies, and rituals of daily life. Stone arrangements may be small and easily moved from place to place, or they may be larger, with stones embedded in the soil. Some represent fishing boats, whereas others are concentric circles with larger stones aligned to the cardinal directions (east, west, north, south), or important constellations in the night sky.

Native Australian people have carved wood throughout their history. Although the Australian climate is generally dry, few ancient wood sculptures survive. Carving styles used natural wood shapes to create images of animals, people, and ancestral spirits.

Burrup rock art found in Deep George, Australia.

An aboriginal mask.

Aboriginal wood, called *punu*, were used for many purposes, from storytelling to spiritual ceremonies. Aboriginal people also use hollow, carved, and painted logs for burial ceremonies. Unused examples of hollow-log bone coffins are exhibited at the National Gallery of Australia as the Aboriginal Memorial, established in 1988. Each bone coffin represents the life of an indigenous person who lost his or her life defending the land after the arrival of British colonists in 1788.

Contemporary aboriginal artists have begun to create artwork that is increasing in value to worldwide art collectors and museums. Contemporary aboriginal sculptures may be made of wood, fiber, or stone. Australia's Parliament House in Canberra has a boomerang-shaped forecourt that includes a mosaic by the indigenous artist Michael Nelson Tjakamarra called *Possum and Wallaby Dreaming*.

INDONESIA: HOME OF THE WORLD'S TALLEST VIRGIN MARY

Indonesia comprises more than 18,000 islands, which are home to more than 260 million people. It is the world's fourth most populous nation and is diverse in history, culture, and religious traditions. Indonesia's many islands host nearly as many art traditions, including many types of sculpture. Some of the best known islands in Indonesia are Bali, Borneo, Java, and Sumatra.

Various religions have inspired many of Indonesia's monumental sculptures. The tallest statue of the Virgin Mary in the world is located on the island of Semarang, based on an original found in Bulgaria. The statue is made of a mixture of sand and resin on a steel frame, and it is painted in lifelike colors, apart from a batik pattern on Mary's hands and blue cloak. Batik is a fabric-dying technique that uses wax and dye to create an intricate geometric pattern.

The statue of Mother Mary in Semerang is the tallest in the world.

The largest sleeping Buddha in the world, at a length of 72 feet (22 m), is a gold-covered statue in East Java. Buddha's face is peaceful, and his resting pose is graceful. The sculptor I Wayan Winten created a dramatic scene of the hero Ghatotkacha at Bali's international airport that commemorates a scene from the Hindu epic the *Mahabharata*.

Indonesia produces many of the world's most valuable and exotic woods, including teak, mahogany, rosewood, and acacia. These woods are used worldwide for furnishings and decor, as well as fine wood carving. I Wayan Winten creates many smaller wood sculptures from fine Indonesian woods.

Contemporary Indonesian sculptors use nearly every material available to them to construct innovative three-dimensional art. Mulyana created a complete underwater world out of crocheted fibers, including fish, sponges, coral, and a kelp forest, which was exhibited at Indonesia's Art Jog in 2018. Heri Dono forms large moveable metal and wood sculptures that comment on social and political issues, including a playful, yet vaguely menacing, metal dinosaur on toy wooden wheels.

Contemporary Indonesian sculptor Heri Dono's metal dinosaur on toy wooden wheels.

POLYNESIA'S WELL-TRAVELED SCULPTURE TRADITIONS

Polynesia means "many islands" in Greek, and the term is accurate: Polynesia includes more than 1,000 islands in the Pacific Ocean, from Hawaii in the north to the largest Polynesian island, New Zealand, in the south. Tonga, Samoa, Easter Island (Rapa Nui), and Tahiti are all islands in Polynesia.

Polynesian people came from Southeast Asia about 3,000 years ago and, starting with Samoa, settled throughout the other Pacific islands, ending with New Zealand in approximately 1300 CE. An early petroglyph found on Tahiti illustrates the type of wood canoe created with stone, bone, and coral tools that Polynesian voyagers used to discover and settle islands throughout the Pacific. The same

The moai statues on Easter Island are a UNESCO World Heritage site.

Polynesian tiki carved artwork.

tools that Polynesian voyagers used to create their canoes and outriggers were used to carve stone and wood statues and monuments.

Strong candidates for the most famous Polynesian sculptures of all time are the *moai* of Easter Island (Rapa Nui). The *moai* represented the ancestors of the Rapa Nui people and were quarried out of gray and red volcanic rock. The tallest *moai* ever created was 33 feet (10 m) tall and weighed 90 tons. *Moai* were erected on large plinths (stone platforms) and featured red topknots indicating hair styles. Their eyes were created by coral and obsidian or red volcanic stone. Some *moai* were painted, and chieftains competed in prestige by creating the largest, grandest *moai*.

Polynesians also created smaller statues and figurines from wood and stone. In addition to the tiki, who can represent the first man or an ancestor, other carvings include depictions of gods, including A'a and Kane.

Who Is the Tiki?

Tiki means "man" or "first man" in most Polynesian languages. In New Zealand, tiki are small and sculpted from greenstone and worn around the neck. Tikis may represent ancestors or the myth of Tiki, the first man created by the god Tane. Larger Maori tikis could represent the creators of different animals and humans. Hawaiian tikis may be made of wood or stone and can be small or large. Tikis in Hawaii may be carved from trees, resulting in a tall standing wood sculpture like a totem pole. Hawaiian tikis can represent Ku, the god of war; Kane, the god of creation; Kanaloa, the god of the sea; or Lono, the god of peace. Tikis seen in American "tiki bars" are a visual imitation of original Hawaiian or Maori tikis and don't represent any god, ancestor, or ideal.

Carved wood male and female Tiki god statues on a beach in Hawaii.

MAORI CARVING: THE HEART OF POLYNESIAN SCULPTURE

Although New Zealand was the last island to be settled by Polynesians, it is considered the heart of sculpture in the South Pacific. The art of sculpture is called *whakairo* by Maori, and it includes carving wood, bone, or stone. The most common type of stone used by Maori is greenstone, a hard native New Zealand semiprecious stone. Maori carvers create their works of art for spiritual and aesthetic (visual) reasons. Intricate, detailed wood carvings are found inside and outside of Maori homes and buildings.

Maori artists intend to make their carvings look so alive that they could almost move and speak. Maori architectural carvings of doors, lintels, and columns illustrate myths and legends. The Maori experienced a cultural renaissance during the twentieth century, and there are now many Maori artists creating art inspired by traditional and forward-looking aspects of their history, language, and culture.

A traditional Maori whakairo wood carving.

THE MASSIVE *MOAI* OF EASTER ISLAND (RAPA NUI)

Located more than 2,000 miles (3,500 km) west of Chile, Easter Island is considered the most remote inhabited island in the world. The island is called Rapa Nui by native Polynesians, who arrived around 1200 CE. Easter Island is a World Heritage site because of the *moai*, large statues commemorating the island's ancestors. More than 900 *moai* have been found on Easter Island. They are carved from gray volcanic tuff, a soft stone that is relatively easy to quarry. As many as 150 people may have been required to move the massive statues from their quarries to display platforms (*ahu*) located on the coast.

In the 1800s, the island's population suffered from starvation and social decline, and the Rapa Nui people toppled all of the *moai* during a period of unrest. In recent years, however, a number of the *moai* have been restored. A restored platform at Ahu Tongariki shows how the monuments may have originally looked, including one *moai* with a red volcanic stone topknot, or *pukao*.

Moai have been restored on a platform at Ahu Tongariki.

PAPUA NEW GUINEA SCULPTURE

Papua New Guinea (PNG) is the eastern half of the island of New Guinea, located north of Australia in the Southwest Pacific. The western half of the island, Papua, is part of Indonesia. People settled Papua New Guinea approximately 45,000 years ago and are among the most ancient indigenous people known today. Their land is one of the most diverse and ecologically rich regions on earth.

Over 800 languages are spoken in PNG, and many of its tribes have limited contact with the outside world. A sculpture garden at Stanford University in Palo Alto, California, showcases some of the sculpture of the island, created in 1994 by 10 woodcarvers who came from villages of the Iatmul and Kwoma people. Sculptures produced by the men include a soaring armored eagle, a thin-legged Tiki-like grinning ancestor, and tall spirit/ancestor poles.

The mudmen of Papua New Guinea.

NAPOLEON ABUEVA: "THE FATHER OF MODERN PHILIPPINE SCULPTURE"

Napoleon Abueva is a renowned sculptor from the Philippines who died at age 88 in February 2018. Abueva is regarded as the "Father of Modern Philippine Sculpture" because of his many contributions to the country's cultural heritage. People first arrived in the Philippines at least 67,000 years ago, and the islands became a Spanish colony after the visit of Ferdinand Magellan in 1521. Napoleon Abueva's art reflects Spanish and precolonial influences on Filipino culture. His sculpture *Siyam na Diwata ng Sining* represents nine fairies of the theater and is exhibited in a sculpture garden at the University of the Philippines College of Arts and Letters in Quezon City.

Napolean Abueva's Three Women Sewing the Filipino Flag.

MANGAREVAN WOOD CARVINGS

Mangarevan artists sculpted expressive and simple tiki (male) representations of gods and ancestors for hundreds of years. Mangareva, or Maareva, is one of the Gambier Islands in French Polynesia, and today about 1,200 people live there. Mangarevan people developed a binary numbering system in 1450 CE, about 300 years before a similar system was invented in Europe. Mangarevan wood carvings are simple and elegant in form, with their own distinctive look that differs from many other Polynesian sculptures. The figures are among the rarest and most desirable of Polynesian carvings today, because the majority were burned in 1835 at the request of European missionaries.

A Mangarevan wood carving.

A FAMOUS POLYNESIAN IDOL: THE GOD A'A

A'a as a name for a god is known only on the small island of Rurutu. In 1821 a famous example of A'a was presented to British missionaries by the people of Rurutu, the most northerly island in French Polynesia. The A'a figure is now exhibited at the British Museum in London. It was probably created between 1500 and 1600 CE and held sacred items. It was made of sandalwood, a fragrant wood not found on Rurutu, and the figure's hollow body also contained a red feather from a lorikeet (a small parrot-like bird) from a neighboring island, which meant it was made from rare and highly desirable materials.

The state of A'a in the British Museum.

A traditional canoe made with Hawaiian koa.

POLYNESIAN AND INDONESIAN WOODS

Tropical island climates and vast geographic distances contributed to the exotic wood from trees found on Polynesian islands, from Hawaii to French Polynesia and New Zealand. Pacific and oceanic rosewood are hard, fine-grained red woods that are suitable for many types of carving and polishing. Hawaiian koa is a large, tall tree with very hard wood that is used for carving jewelry and furniture. Other types of Polynesian wood include avocado, lychee, coconut, and monkey pod. Indonesian woods that are used for carving and furniture-making around the world include mahogany, teak, rosewood, and acacia.

FURTHER READING & INTERNET RESOURCES

BOOKS

Brinkmann, Vinzenz, Renee Dreyfus, and Ulrike Koch-Brinkmann, eds. *Gods in Color: Polychromy in the Ancient World*. Munich, Germany: Prestel, 2017.

Kinoshita, Hiromi, ed. *Art of China: Highlights from the Philadelphia Museum of Art*. New Haven, CT: Yale University Press, 2018.

Kuhtz, Cleo. *Sculpture: Materials, Techniques, Styles, and Practice*. New York: Rosen Education Service, 2016.

Schimmel, Paul, ed. *Revolution in the Making: Abstract Sculpture by Women, 1940–2006*. Milan: Skira, 2016.

Tolles, Thayer. *The American West in Bronze, 1850–1925*. New York: Metropolitan Museum of Art, 2014.

WEB SITES

https://www.artic.edu/collection. The online catalog of the Art Institute of Chicago's official art collection.

www.metmuseum.org/toah/. The Metropolitan Museum of Art's Heilbrunn Timeline of Art History.

news.artnet.com. News and updates on the world of fine art from ArtNet.

http://www.visual-arts-cork.com. An independent online visual arts encyclopedia, with over 5,000 images.

www.smarthistory.org. Smarthistory is a free open-source art history partner of Khan Academy, founded by Dr. Beth Harris and Dr. Steven Zucker.

INDEX

AUTHOR'S BIOGRAPHY

Amy Sterling Casil has an MFA from Chapman University and a bachelor's degree in studio art from Scripps College. She teaches at Saddleback College in Mission Viejo, CA, and has published more than 25 books for school classrooms and libraries, as well as award-winning fiction.

CREDITS

COVER

(clockwise from top left) Jade Buddha, China, Davide Ferdinando Precone/Dreamstime; Acropolis, Greece, Vangelis Aragiannis/Dreamstime; *Maori* carving, New Zealand, Dreamstime; first-century statues, Turkey, MehmetO/Shutterstock; Flamingo by Alexander Calder, Chicago, James Kirkikis/Dreamstime; El Gato by Botero, Barcelona, Spain, Oleksandr Rogovyy/Dreamstime

INTERIOR

1, Busara/Shutterstock; 2-3, naipung/Shutterstock; 5, DR Travel Photo and Video/Shutterstock; 9, Tatiana Akhmetgalieva/Shutterstock; 10, Louvre Museum/Wikimedia Commons; 11, British Museum/Wikimedia Commons; 12, I, Sailko/Wikimedia Commons; 13, Bin im Garten/Wikimedia Commons; 14, africa924/Shutterstock; 15, Henk Paul/Shutterstock; 16, WaynaQhapaq/Wikimedia Commons; 17, Carolus Ludovicus/Wikimedia Commons; 18, Alan Gignoux/Dreamstime; 19 UP, Louvre Museum [Public domain]; 19 LO, Nnenna Okore/Wikimedia Commons; 20 UP, Karen Green; 20 LO, Kiev.Victor/Shutterstock; 21, Godruma/iStock; 22, kool99/iStock; 23, 4X-image/iStock; 24, Martin Silva Cosentino/Dreamstime; 25, steve estvanik/Shutterstock; 26, Jen with modifications by Ismoon 20 February 2012 (earlier version by Calliopejen1)/Wikimedia Commons; 27, dreamloveyou/Shutterstock; 28, Zhenshan Zhou/Dreamstime; 29, 56733678/Dreamstime; 30, Guimet Museum/Wikimedia Commons; 31 UP, cowardlion/Shutterstock; 31 LO, Tea/Dreamstime; 32 UP, Ken Taylor/Dreamstime; 32 LO, Lord Jim; 33, Terriana/Dreamstime; 34, Sergio Bertino/Dreamstime; 35, Marcovarro/Dreamstime; 36, Gerard M (at Dutch Wikipedia)/Wikimedia Commons; 37, Euriico/Dreamstime; 38, Claudio Giovanni Colombo/Dreamstime; 39, magann/iStock; 40, Neil Harrison/Dreamstime; 41, Michael Foy/Dreamstime; 42, S-F/Shutterstock; 43 UP, Rramirez125/Dreamstime; 43 LO, I, VollwertBIT/Wikimedia Commons; 44 UP, gracemenicholson/iStock; 44 LO, Veniamin Kraskov/Dreamstime; 45, SongSpeckles/iStock; 46, Album/Metropolitan Museum of Art, NY/Newscom; 47, Mihail Ivanov/Dreamstime; 48, simonmayer/iStock; 49, SEYLUL06/iStock; 50, Fer Gregory/Shutterstock; 51, Jesus Eloy Ramos Lara/Dreamstime; 52, Jesus Eloy Ramos Lara/Dreamstime; 53, SL-Photograhy/Shutterstock; 54, Wuttichai jantarak/Shutterstock; 55 UP, Rodrigolab/Dreamstime; 55 LO, Régis Lachaume/Wikimedia Commons; 56 UP, Atosan/Dreamstime; 56 LO, CB2/ZOB/BREEF/Newscom; 57, Morphart Creation/Shutterstock; 58, ivanadb/iStock; 59, Adam Jan Figel/Shutterstock; 60, Wikimedia Commons; 61, efesenko/iStock; 62, Inspired By Maps/Shutterstock; 63, Murat Tellioglu/Dreamstime; 64, eFesenko/Shutterstock; 65, Ramillah/Dreamstime; 66, Mihail Ivanov/Dreamstime; 67 UP, Nader Elsawaf/Dreamstime; 67 LO, MehmetO/Shutterstock; 68 UP, Louvre Museum/Wikimedia Commons; 68 LO, Gary Lee/Photoshot/Newscom; 69, millerium arkay/Shutterstock; 70, Eric Ewing/Wikimedia Commons; 71, CWLawrence/iStock; 73, Andrius Kaziliunas/iStock; 74, Charles Marion Russell/Wikimedia Commons; 75, Frederic Remington/Wikimedia Commons; 76, Louise Rivard/Dreamstime; 77, Erin Alexis Randolph/Dreamstime; 78, Meunierd/Dreamstime; 79 UP, Joyce Nelson/Shutterstock; 79 LO, Louise Rivard/Dreamstime; 80 UP, Demerzel21/Dreamstime; 80 LO, Eric Broder Van Dyke/Dreamstime; 81, Yehor Vlasenko/Dreamstime; 82, Marco Tomasini/Dreamstime; 83, Liverbird/Dreamstime; 84, Budidhoni/Dreamstime; 85, Felix Hrhager/dpa/picture-alliance/Newscom; 86, lovelypeace/iStock; 87, jimkruger/iStock; 88, Terrence Kuiper/Dreamstime; 89, chameleonseye/iStock; 90, EdoTealdi/iStock; 91, Stanislav Solovkin/Dreamstime; 92 UP, Manolito Tiuseco/Shutterstok; 92 LO, Cliff/Wikimedia Commons; 93 UP, Internet Archive Book Images/Wikimedia Commons; 93 LO, Theodore Trimmer/Shutterstock